MW00872621

MITCH TAEBEL

LOOKING OUT FOR AMERICA

SYNOPSIS

This Memoir and political Manifesto is about my Success in Entertainment in Los Angeles and Manhattan, Travels around the World, Corruption in Government, History, Law and sex. This Book is about changing the World and for the Better. The Public has a Civic Duty to address the issues covered and not to tolerate unlawful conduct by government especially when Aired on National Television.

PREFACE

In search of sanctity one must use experience and intuition to prevail one's purpose in life, generally being the enjoyment of the overall experience, what that entails is up to the individual.

INTRODUCTION

I am a TV Host, Presenter, Actor, Journalist, Winner of multiple Film Awards, Photographer, Author, Innovator, Entrepreneur, Philanthropist, Comedian, legal and political Connoisseur. I usually have at least two girls around me wherever go at all times. I'm famous and I can't stand it when people don't know who I am. I was cast as the most interesting man in the world. I will make this the most interesting Book in the World. In 2010 at the age of twenty three I moved to Los Angeles and began a career in Entertainment. In the first year and a half I booked over seven commercials and worked on dozens of film and TV productions. I was Elected hundreds of times against Billions of Competitors by Producers, Directors, Production Companies and Talent Agencies. I was more successful than most A-list Actors my first year in Entertainment because at that age I was better looking than all of them. In 2017 I also won two Film Awards. I am an IGFA World Record holder since 1999. In 2018 I attended Arizona State University for Film and Media Production. In 2007 I traveled around the world on Semester At Sea through University of Virginia. In 2010 I Attained a Degree from Colorado Mountain College. I've always thought I was destined to be President of The United States. I had a public service para transit job in College. I became very opinionated after listening to a lot of political talk radio, reading the newspaper and a few books. Later began to read law starting with The Declaration of Independence, U.S. Constitution and the First Acts of Congress. I became motivated to write a Book when my credibility and competence were challenged on National TV when I was kidnapped by police in Arizona after filing several lawsuits. I think the smarter people are the more they will be able to appreciate this story. John Lewis was arrested forty times before he was Elected to Congress. Even a felon has an absolute right to run for President of the United States. The charges in Arizona were dismissed. This Book is about saving lives. It is mostly for the Libertarians, Constitutionalists and Republicans although I agree with a few liberal views. It's about public Awareness. I want to party with Celebrities and I want a better Talent Agency. Everyone has Civic Duty to read this book. Maybe you're reading to see what I have to say after a 60 mile slow-speed police pursuit with three helicopters across Phoenix in defense of Your Constitutional Rights and a Press statement that I made viewed by Tens of Millions of People Defending the Constitution. Commentators said I was a "Future Senator", "right", "spot on", "True Patriot" and a "Hero". The first thing I ask is that you share this Book with at least few people. It is about saving this Country and the World that follows. Your invited to write to the media and tell them they should to cover both sides of this story better or to the U.S. Government and tell them they should enforce the Civil Rights Act. Part of being a conscious and good human being is understanding what evil wants and doing the opposite. Life for a man is about standing his ground and the World depends on Men who do. You are invited to defend Freedom of Speech and common sense in social media. Most of what was written online was the result of a Media Preclusion order and before I wrote this Book and made my Facebook photo albums public. I put a little sex in my Book. I hope you find this story compelling. Talking about All This Love making is called a Freedom of Speech. Liberty starts Now! This is no ordinary book. The Theme is comprised of every word front to back. I will start with my Autobiography skip to chapter four if you want to start with the kidnapping in Arizona. I get my kicks through working in Entertainment and prefer to work virtually 100% of the time however I've faced some major setbacks due to our problem with a rogue criminal justice system with crooked homosexuals that do everything backwards. I like to work with people every day all day. Dating girls is part of being an Actor. Whether Acting, Producing a film, talking to hot girls, Networking, teaching an Acting Class, doing a Photo Shoot or hitting the gym I'm working. I would like to have a lot of kids and work a bit less in the future but for the time being it's great. I want to live in the United States half the time. I affirmed through Acting, girls, Boxing, Film Making, and now Law that you are reading the Memoir of a Genius like the World has never seen before. I also took an IQ Test. Though it does not measure Creative ability, work Ethic, Social Skills or any of my best endowments. There is absolutely no reason I shouldn't have made at least tens of millions by now other than a few disgusting liberals who infiltrated the Justice system. I also recently took a memory test and scored in the 1st percentile. My civic duties are off the charts. The world needs my problem solving abilities. I'm happy to prove it. Just offer me an internship with your company, in The White House or on a campaign. I Aced Senior Literature in High School and English Comp II in College but more importantly I have a lot to say. I've thought I should be President of The United States since I was a Freshman in High School and now I'm positive. I have witnessed such shortfalls from both the government and Media I now am now sure. I pledge to give 33% of all my proceeds from the lawsuits I've filed to Charity. The money will go at least 300% further in my hands therefore it wont cost the public anything. I'm not obsessed with myself, I'm obsessed with girls and having a good time. There are just some things I really like and some things I don't like that's just part of being an exceptional Human Being. I think Seth Meyers, Stephen Colbert, Ryan Seacrest, Carson Daly, Conan O'Brien and Joe Rogan are all tremendously talented. I support Liberty, Pursuit of Happiness and Privacy from government. I usually agree with the Republicans on Most issues and Democrats on others. My favorite Book is the World Almanac. I believe the wisdom in our Declaration of Independence and the United States Constitution can solve all the problems in this country. The government serves no other purpose than to support our right to Pursuit of Happiness. Girls tell me I'm the funniest guy they've ever met. If you spend time reading spend time reading law. Knowledge is power. We can still have a sense of humor despite much of this Book having very serious subject matter. Now lets save the World and make this a panty dropper. Aside from during and after two times

I've unlawfully been in jail I Always look like a Fitness Model or a Doctor who takes care of himself. I have Four Websites, an IMDB with six Directing and Producing credits, five Social Networking sites and Vimeo and Youtube channels, See WWW.MITCHTAEBEL.COM. The view counts may or may not be accurate. I invite you to ask questions and make comments on social media after reading this. Everyone is invited to subscribe to my Channels and follow me on Twitter. If I gave you my business card definitely friend request me on Facebook. My maxims are most of the worlds problems are due to misconceptions, treat everyone like a business partner or voter and Liberty must constantly be defended from stupid. When it comes to government Monkey see Monkey do. I wouldn't say that if they were actually helping because that would be the ethical thing to do. I am the only person on the internet probably in the world with my name. The Declaration of Independence describes many of the reasons we fought a war for freedom and independence, among them were arbitrary government, obstruction of justice, officer harassment, charges for pretend offenses and abuse of discretion by the courts described as mock trials. These were some of the primary reasons so many Europeans risked their lives to sail across the seas to settle on a new continent. It also clearly declares the purpose of government is to aid our "safety and happiness". I'm like Albert Einstein when it comes to Pursuit of Happiness. Sometimes think I am the only one with any enthusiasm. I am an advocate of the 1st Amendment in the Bill of Rights. Freedom of speech, assembly and right to take anyone to court before a jury of citizens for violating a person's rights is essential to any modern Free Society. Freedom of expression is a right guaranteed by the 1st Amendment of the U.S. Constitution and is an explicit right of the European Convention on Human Rights Act of 1998 in §1.7.2(f) of Article 10. The freedom of the press is essential to our "Republican form of government" as declared in Article

IV section IV of the U.S. Constitution. A Republic is legally defined as "a system of government in which the people hold sovereign power and elect representatives who exercise that power.", See Black's Law Dictionary, West Publishing Co. (2016). The Supreme Court has stated in many ways, the freedom of the press is the "constitutionally chosen means for keeping officials elected by the people responsible to all the people whom they were selected to serve.", See Mills v. Alabama, 384 U.S. 214 (1966). The fundamental priority for every person should be Pursuit of Happiness without infringing upon the rights of others, which is central to the philosophy of the founding fathers. This concept was essentially ratified in the Ninth Amendment and is paramount for the well being of any society. "The constitutional guarantee of a free press assures the maintenance of our political system and an open society.", See Pell v. Procunier, 417 U.S. 817 (1974); quoting Time, Inc. v. Hill, 385 U.S. 374 (1967). Here, The Supreme Court "discussed the role of the media as a powerful antidote to any abuses of power by government officials", See Houchins v. KQED, Inc., 438 U.S. 1 (1978). The Supreme Court has also stated, "any system of prior restraints of expression comes to this court bearing a heavy presumption against it's constitutional validity.", See New York Times Co. v. United States, 403 U.S. 713 (1971). Like the Celebrities I've met most of these cases can be found in a Yahoo, Bing or Google search. For U.S. Supreme Court law I enter the name of the case and maybe the year then space "find" space "law" and in search results you can usually find the ruling on caselaw.findlaw.com which seems to be reliable. For U.S. Circuit Law, U.S. District Law and state rulings you will want to enter as much of the legal citation as you have in a search engine. I provide full citations for all cases cited. WestLaw.com or LexisNexis.com also work but are used by law firms and may be expensive. I use Oyez to see how each of the judges ruled. Pacer.gov can be used to access all federal lawsuits I have filed. The right to pursue happiness is an absolute right founded in The Declaration of Independence and is supported by law in many ways. My legal dictionary has one definition, "The constitutional right to pursue any lawful business or activity that might yield the highest enjoyment, increase one's prosperity, or allow the development of one's faculties as long as it is not inconsistent with others rights", See Black's Law Dictionary, West Publishing Co. (2016). The key to happiness is to live by one's will with the consent of others. Art is an expression of self and feeling which is timeless. Few are fortunate enough to make a prosperous living by artistic innovation and expression however it's a way of life I have chosen and I'm willing to work much harder than most people. Law is the basis of government. Legal fundamentals must be a prerequisite to a high school diploma. A state or federal license should not be required to practice law. Why have we deviated from the wisdom of the framers of the country who understood life under arbitrary power? In the First Congress, Chapter XX Section 35 states "that in all courts of The United States, the parties may plead and manage their own causes personally or by the assistance of such counsel or attorneys at law". I advocate legal knowledge by the general public as it is the most pragmatic way to seek resolution, defend yourself and your rights, keep the government in check and as the President's Oath states in Article II Section I of The U.S. Constitution, "preserve, protect and defend the Constitution of The United States". First Congress Chapter XX Section 9 states that the U.S. District Courts only have the authority to impose "a term of imprisonment not exceeding six months". For profit corporations have been involving themselves in state governments and law enforcement to the extent it has degraded our entire justice system. In November of 2017 I sent letters to all fifty governors regarding the direction of this country and asked them to forward the letters to all the state legislators. I heard back only from the Illinois governor Bruce Rauner. I asked to meet with state legislators regarding an Article V state convention. I originally drafted a book in the Phoenix jail. I was kidnapped by police and unlawfully detained by a tyrannical government. Detained for over three years without due process of law before the charges were eventually dismissed April 9th 2021. This Book is much better. It was an example of what excessive government leads to. Four of the past seven Illinois Governors spent time in prison. This travesty of justice is a facet of a much bigger problem on a Federal level and state level. Everyone in this Country has an Constitutional Right to Release on Bail if they are arrested. This book covers much of what I studied while detained. It contains a lot of facts and anecdotes. I read more law in that time than most lawyers read in law school. You don't have to be a lawyer to understand this Book and you will know more than most lawyers after reading it. Most lawyers are so stupid and know so little about law it's mind blowing. The best of the best should agree with me. I'm apparently like William Blackstone. Four states California, Virginia, Vermont, Washington, Wyoming, New York and Maine do not require aspiring lawyers have a law degree prior to becoming a lawyer. A Federal judge is not required to have a degree and only twenty eight states require judges to have a law degree. Furthermore anyone can represent themselves as a Plaintiff or defendant any time in state or Federal Court. I was protesting an illegal vehicle stop and law enforcement used excessive force which instigated a high speed pursuit and accident. Prior to being assaulted by police I was doing the speed limit and stopping at red lights. If Martin Luther King Jr. and Rosa Parks can be respected for breaking the law I should certainly be respected for lawfully protesting a kidnapping. I called the Media, 911, the Phoenix Mayor and Face timed Raquel T. during the sixty mile slow-speed pursuit. I stated to Fox News over the phone that officers would be "sued and prosecuted" if they proceeded to make an unlawful arrest. At least three Helicopters covered the slow-speed pursuit that lasted an hour. Arizona police deployed seven spike strips on the highway for my refusal to stop which I avoided. Spike strips at highway speeds are technically "deadly force" and the use of deadly force was unlawful, See Tennessee v. Garner, 471 U.S. 1 (1985); U.S. v. Pineda-Doval, 614 F.3d 1019 (9th Cir. 2010); Orn v. City of Tacoma, 949 F.3d 1167 (9th Cir. 2020). The homosexual aliens that like to control government were embarrassed and they have been retaliating ever since getting people to write obscenely stupid comments on YouTube. Law enforcement did Not use deadly force against O.J. Simpson in 1994 during that police pursuit and they had a warrant for murder. It was one of the most watched cases in history and he didn't make a press statement defending himself. When someone is arrested and wants to give a public statement on camera the public should give them the benefit of the doubt if they are saying they are innocent because they are obviously not afraid of being caught in a lie. I felt like I had at that point gone to extreme lengths not to endanger any other drivers. The use of spike strips was arguably seven counts of "attempted murder" by officers, See 18 U.S.C. §1113 or seven counts of "use, attempted use, or threatened use of a dangerous weapon" in addition to "Kidnapping" in violation of 18 U.S.C. §241 & §242; 18 U.S.C. §1201. This proves law enforcement in Arizona are insane and dangerous. It promotes excessive force and other unlawful conduct by officers not to prosecute them for it. The government allowed the officers to make a BIG example of how they can get away with committing felonies on TV by use of unjustified deadly force and kidnapping with excessive bail. Failure to prosecute them or even describe the conduct as assault created very bias media coverage and was thus a violation of due process and the basis for malicious prosecution. I feel like an African-American in the sixties living for Pursuit of Happiness and getting attacked for it. At least one of the helicopters covered the unlawful use of several of the spike strips early in the pursuit. And the officer's dangerous attempt to throw a spike strip out of his window at 75 mph was captured on camera. I've seen the video. Despite prosecution being barred by law, I was unconstitutionally arrested. One witness isn't enough to prosecute someone law enforcement always needs corroborating evidence to protect the public from unjustified arrests. The "two-witness rule" has been around for thousands of years and is in the Holly Bible, See Deuteronomy 19:15; Numbers 35:30. It's in the U.S. Constitution, See Art. III Sec. 3. It's in the Legal Dictionary. It is in other words in U.S. Supreme Court Law, See Jones v. U.S., 362 U.S. 257 (1960). It would completely defeat the protections of due process of law if a single lying witness could convict someone beyond a reasonable doubt of an alleged crime without corroborating evidence. "Obviously, however, one cannot be punished for failing to obey the command of an officer if that command is itself violative of the constitution.", See Wainwright v. City of New Orleans, 392 U.S. 598 (1968) (Douglas); quoting Wright v. Georgia, 373 U.S. 284 (1963). You can review the Media and Youtube comments after reading this Book and you will understand I have faced a plague of idiots. People are so stupid every where I look they minds well wear their pants backwards. I hope it will be impossible for anyone who reads this book to be one of those people. Please share the book with family and friends. Law enforcement in the U.S. average about six months of training where officers across Europe average about three years. Arizona does Not require their city or state police to have college Degrees like many states. I'm too smart to have to done anything illegal. Under the Sherman-Sorrells Doctrine charges cannot be pressed because I was not "predisposed" to refuse an officer's illegal order or have an accident, in other words the accident was instigated and caused by law enforcement, See U.S. v. Russell, 411 U.S. 423 (1973). The police department that made the assaults and unlawful arrest makes nineteen unlawful arrests without probable cause per day and then get sued and pay damages to all the victims of unlawful arrest, See United Steelworkers of America v. Milstead, 705 F.Supp. 1426 United States District Court, D. Arizona (1988). The First Circuit Affirmed $100,000,000 for False Imprisonment and the victim was probably a career criminal, See Limone v. Condon, 372 F.3d 39 (1st Cir. 2004). The United Nation's Code of Conduct for Law Enforcement Officials states "Law Enforcement officials may use force only when strictly necessary". Officers were in violation of pursuit standards across the country and U.S. Supreme Court Law. After the unconstitutional arrest I asked to speak with the Arizona Attorney General, however, the request was denied. Instead they alleged I was delusional like law enforcement has been known to do against perfectly stable people, See Wagenmann v. Adams, 829 F.2d 196 (1st Cir. 1987). That County acts as if they can't tell the difference between crazy and smart crazy. I met a lawyer and an accountant with a masters degree who were both in the Arizona rule 11 competency evaluation. All the smart people were in competency evaluation. Government can't call people crazy because they feel stupid. I had tried to bring as much attention to the fact I was being unlawfully arrested and kidnapped by calling the Media from the Highway and making a fifteen minute press statement the next morning. I had already been on National Television a number of times on a in Commercials and on a Court TV show. I also had already done a fifteen minute Lecture on the web about the Declaration of Independence and Constitution. This was the first time someone made a press statement reporting they were kidnapped by law enforcement especially after a 60 mile slow-speed pursuit. I almost stated that I wanted to run for President and regret not doing so. If I knew that was going to be the only press conference I definitely would have. You have to Rise Above stupid. The Press statement would have been a hundred times better had I not spent the night in jail.

I should be one of the most famous people in the world right now. I voted for Donald Trump and his tax cuts. One thing he didn't do well was allow this assault and kidnapping and fail to enforce the Civil Rights Act. The press conference is on YouTube. I am NOT a sovereign citizen I had no idea what that journalist was talking about. I had no idea what kind of stupidity that term associated with. I was informed that Fox News, ABC, NBC, CBS Arizona Family and UNIDAD were all present and CNN did cover the story and play my press statement six days later. So did Sean Hannity and Fox News. The law enforcement in response refused to ever talk about whether the arrest was lawful or not and then got an unconstitutional court order to keep the press from talking to me until the case was resolved. They have still to this day refused to ever have a legal discussion about the force used and the illegality of the arrest. I expected an on going debate to take place about what happened however they kept me detained by unconstitutional excessive bail and got the media preclusion order. What the law is and what these people are doing are two different things. They are either very stupid reckless and unaware that everything they are doing is illegal or it was an intentional kidnapping and Conspiracy against my rights, See 18 U.S.C. §371; 18 U.S.C. §241. I would like to see what a prevailing lawsuit will uncover. This book is in part a response to the Media coverage. Depending on what happens moving forward, it could be proof that we have a tyrannical government and controlled media or hopefully not. The courts have dismissed most of the lawsuits I've filed without even requiring the defendants to admit or deny the allegations. All valid lawsuits. As an Award Winning political Filmmaker and a college graduate I should be considered more credible than any police officer and should have immediately been released. If I had written a book already I would like to think I never would have spent a day in jail. I have now filed over twenty lawsuits against the state officials demanding

Injunctive relief and monetary damages of over $1 trillion. In the great America no one can tell you to slow down when you're playing by the rules or doing the speed limit. Life is like a sports game. No one can tell you, you're enjoying life too much. This book will rock the earth like a meteor. If you bought this book you are a patriot. Here is a short Autobiography and Manifesto.

CHAPTER 1

I was born in Chicago, IL September 1st 1986 on Labor Day to a stock broker and a school teacher. My father studied finance and graduated with a bachelors from Colorado he worked at Morgan Stanley for over twenty years. My mother graduated with a political science degree from St. Mary's College. She was prom queen in High school. I am named after my uncle Mitch Stoltz who was pitcher and Captain of the Notre Dame Baseball team. He knew Dan Quayle before he was Vice President of the United States. My mother's maiden name is Stoltz. I am related to Eric Stoltz the Actor, Producer and Director. I am related to The Stewarts by first maternal grandmother Colleen Stewart. I think I'm related to Martha Stewart. I am related to Judge Potter Stewart of The Supreme Court of The United States. I am related to the Stones by first paternal grandmother Mildred Stone. I am related to Biz Stone who co-founded twitter and Emma Stone the Actress. I am related to Oliver Stone one of the greatest Film Director Producers of all time. I am from a family in the top 1% that pay the most taxes and help the world most. It is important to me to associate with the High Achievers of the World. I am related to Thomas Stone the Lawyer from Maryland who signed the Declaration of Independence and Chief Judge Harlan F. Stone of The Supreme Court of The United

States. I am related to The Roe and Cass families through my great grandparents. My great great grandfather Augusta Taebel started a Church in Illinois. I am related to the English and German thrones. I am related to John Hancock,President of The Continental Congress. I'm related to Tommy James and the Shondells. There was a sixty bedroom Castle in Germany in my family tree. I'm English, Irish and German.

In 1988 my parents sold the three-flat in Old Town Chicago and bought an acre of property on Lake Michigan in Long Beach, Indiana. I'm from Indiana like James Dean, David Letterman and Abraham Lincoln. I grew up in a house with a three car garage and a swimming pool, tennis court and Jacuzzi in the backyard. The summers were always a lot of fun growing up in a beach town. We met a lot of girls in Bikinis. I grew up around a lot of Millionaires who were friends and clients of my father. Most of them were great people. I was always glad to see friends from Chicago including Kristen and Sean Field, Rob Hearne, Fred Woods, Frank Miulli, ect.. Kristen Field has pictures with Hillary Clinton on Facebook. I hung out with Joe Scartozzi, Michael Macintosh and Sean Wall who lived in the neighborhood. I grew up around Kiva and Dakota Wenig who are jews. Their parents produced an award winning film *Yoga Kids* (1996) with Director Tom McComas and they offered me my first role in a movie. If there was money in it I would have been all over it because Acting and making money is *crème de la crème* as is the U.S. Presidency. Their mother told me I deserve a "Herem". I liked that idea so much I've never been able to get that out of my head. Everything in life has since revolved around getting a Harem in one way or another. I started working out my Biceps at thirteen. I have a younger sister named Marissa Anne Frageman who attained a Master's Degree in social work from Indiana University. I had an adopted half brother named Ryan Taebel who became a police officer. He never lived with us but we would see him on vacation. Before he became a cop he got arrested a few times and got a tattoo. It

14

didn't say protect and serve it abbreviated "fuck the world". He was a bully and seventy five pounds heavier than I was I had to be able to kick his ass to be around him and he had to know it. Then we were friends. Which is exactly how the public should view government. My father's first marriage was to a woman named Linda Edidin. Her father owned Banks in Illinois. I grew up with seven girl cousins. I played soccer in elementary school. We had a black Labrador Retriever and then a Golden Retriever. From an early age I was traveling outside The Country and through many of The States. I spent a number of days fly fishing the tributaries of the Great Lakes. We used to fish with Chad Betts and Jon Kolehouse in Michigan. They are on Youtube. I got into Photography. In 1998 we rented an apartment for two years in Hollywood, Florida on the Intracoastal and a block from the Beach. I would watch Yachts with Helicopters on top go by my window. I enrolled in a middle school known as Summit-Questa owned by Judy Dempsy a friend of my mother. There I learned to date girls, throw a football and type. During lunch every day I played touch football with Daniel Barton, Chris and Mike McMullen and some other guys. I had a six pack at thirteen. I remember having three high school girls that all wanted to suck my dick at the same time but I didn't make it happen. I vowed to not let that happen anymore. The Holy Bible's tradition against premarital sex preceded condoms and birth control. Sex is legal and very ethical. As the Latinos say it is the spice of life. I don't want to loose any Christians. I entertained free diving and saltwater fly fishing in my free time. In 1999 I Certified a Junior and Adult IGFA Fly Fishing World Record with Capt. Mark Giacobba who I had met while doing an internship at Bass Pro Shops and said I was a "Prodigy". Fishing is one of the World's most popular participation sports. If you're not familiar with Fly Fishing, See *A River Runs Through It* (1992). When I was thirteen I hooked up with and fingered a hot Sophomore in high school in my cousins Jacuzzi in Zionsville, IN. My older cousin Kimberly Stoltz Phenicie who later went to Georgetown University and then worked in the CIA said I was "a pimp". From 2000 to 2001 I was home schooled while we traveled around The World. We spent a month on the South Island of New Zealand and a month in Mexico. When I was fourteen I got a blow job from a college girl while staying at a bed and breakfast in New Zealand. She was nineteen. That was also the first time I ever drank alcohol. Then I slept in a bed with her and her girl friend. I was in the middle. We then traveled the North Island of New Zealand, Australia, Tahiti and The British Virgin Islands. I was certified a PADI Scuba Diver in Long Island, Bahamas. In The Bahamas, New Zealand and BVI we spent weeks living aboard sailboats.

The summer before high school I made out with Stacy Robinson and Sunshine Johns in my hot tub. We passed a glow stick around and they tried to get me to go to Marquette High School. But I went to La Lumiere. I was going to be a freshman and I also hooked up with a girl who was going to be a junior named Kelly Holloway before school started. Polygamy is in the Holy Bible, See Genesis 4:19. Charlie Sheen has a "Polygamy Story". Here's a word of advice, never make a woman regret having a threesome. One thing I love about girls is they always like to see me at my best. I bought all equipment and signed up for Martial Arts. When I was growing up people got in fights. It's better to be ahead of the game. I boxed an African-American guy named Eric D. who was going to be a Sophomore and was a Varsity Football Player in public school. I KO ed him with a jab to the face and an unexpected right hook to the abdomen. Misdirection. He got the wind knocked out of him and couldn't get up. Courtney Althoff Ann was my witness. He was one of the first guys I boxed. Later in life I learned that people in Los Angeles and Manhattan don't really fight. I like that better. However in most parts of the country the Alpha has probably been in a fight or two and it would be self-defense. It's an inevitable fact of life that it is better to be able to stand your ground and kick someone's ass when necessary. I got in a few fights keeping dip shits in line.

In the fall of 2001 I enrolled in in a Very Prestigious High School known as La Lumiere in La Porte, Indiana. I played Football in the fall and Baseball in the spring. I wore a Blazer with a tie every day. Some of my colleagues were Libby Shoop Marzotto, Elisse Knoll Ake, Lee Lipniskis, Hillary Gunther Knight, Katie Bankowski Stahoviak, Meghan Sanaghan, James Comstock, James Tungate, Mike Doan, Alex Arnold, Brandon Prough and Mitchell Henderlong. I started Full Body Weight training for Football. I started wrestling competitive wrestlers like Mike Doan on the weekends and beating them. We wrestled to tap out. My favorite move was the Headlock. Arm Bars are good too. We got another black Labrador Retriever a few months old. I was in math class on September 11th when we heard the news of The World Trade Center and Pentagon. The school had also been attended by Chris Farley (Actor), Paris Barclay (Director, Producer), James Christopher Gaffigan (Comedian), John Patrick Hiler (U.S. House Representative), James Banks III (NBA Player), Brian Bowen (NBA Player), Tyler Campbell (Basketball Player), Jaren Walter Jackson Jr. (NBA Player), Jordan Poole (NBA Player), Isaiah Stewart (NBA Player) and Chief Judge of The Supreme Court of The United States John Roberts who is also from my home town of about 1,100 people and was appointed in 2005 by President Bush. I opted to Board with the other students after a month or so. I've been out of the house and living with girls and guys my own age since I was fifteen. Over one of the weekends I had one of my Football teammates named "All Star" over and we both had sex with this hot blond on my basement guest bed. I had sex with her first. All Star who was the smallest guy on the team but a good looking guy came out of the bathroom wearing a condom under his pants ready to have sex. I wear Magnums and that's what I had to give him so the rubber slipped off in his pants and I heard him him say "damn! where's the condom?". After putting on a regular sized condom on he got laid. She was patient. The next week in school we laughed about the story in front of the Seniors and they never looked at us the same way in a good way. I used to get Blow jobs all over campus from this girl named Mallory who had her clit pierced. I let my roommate James Comstock rub her Pussy. I have always had an affinity for fun and easy girls. James once said I was the "voice of reason". That year I studied Theology, Biology, Geography, Spanish, English and Algebra. I got more poontang as a Freshman than any guy in school including all the Seniors. I took the virginity of three girls that year.

In the fall of 2002 attended Marquette Catholic School in Michigan City, IN for a month then transferred to a college prep boarding school outside Sedona, Arizona named Oak Creek Ranch High School where my older adopted brother the police officer went to school. There I met some of my good friends including Katie Wick, Leonna Joy Kommer, David Rich, Jennifer Parker, Blake Mills, J.J. Kim, Carla Milli Siegal, Calvin Peterson, Troy Payne, Sam Scott, Andrew Murray, Ashlin Johnson, Michael Lafevers, Jessica Mahoney, Max Reinhardt, Casey Todd, Bryan Burkhardt, Christopher Brandon Carroll, Shogo Abe, Ryan Berkowitz, Frank Ortega and Kieth Richard Gerdes. Katie Wick was the headmaster's daughter who went to school with us, she has pictures with Presidential Candidate Rick Santorum on Facebook. Frank Ortega (v) has an IMDB. Half of the students were from California. My second week in school a senior came up and pushed on the side of my head with his finger. I asked him if he was trying to fight me. He said "yeah, I'll fight you". I wasn't going to back down and so I got up. He swung first and then I got a hold of him and took him to the ground. I got on top of him and wailed on him from the left and the right. I asked him if we was "done". He just kept saying "get off me" so I hit him again. Then the biggest senior in school pulled me off of him. He didn't try and fight again

18

when he got up. I was a Senior after that and dated the best looking girl in school. In the fall I played flag Football and in the spring I played coed softball. I mostly played Defensive End in High School. I was as fast as anyone on the team and could throw further than the Quarterback. I was completely unaware that I was Bigger than NFL Quarterbacks or maybe I would have prepared for a career in the NFL. Although I'd rather Coach. I later found out Doug Flutie was 5'10" about 170 Lbs. Kyler Murray who is currently the Quarterback for the Cardinals is only 5'10". We used to sneak out of the Movie theater on school trips and fool around with Rachel Ann, Lauren Rodriguez and Sarah Summers who lived in Sedona and went to Red Rock High School. In the spring of 2002 Sophmore year I went to Costa Rica for Spring Break on Outward Bound. I was the only man in a group with five girls. We hiked the rain forests, repelled water falls, went white water rafting and stayed with locals. I also learned to surf. On break before summer school we visited Sun Valley, Idaho and I shot a 12 gauge for the first time with Rian Timmons. A girl that worked at the Phoenix airport thought I was famous. She stopped me and made a big scene as I was about to get on the plane. She thought I was in the Backstreet Boys or NSYNC. She didn't know which band I was in but she was positive I was a Celebrity. Junior year my girlfriend's parents took us to a resort in Puerto Vallarta, Mexico over Christmas break. I went to Park City, Utah on a Snowboard skiing vacation with David Rich our quarterback on Spring Break and we both fucked girls we met. He was two years ahead of me and already in College studying at NAU (Northern Arizona University). In the summer of 2003 I attended Lallapalooza at Grant Park, Chicago with Brett Sima, Phil Wrenn and friends. I went to a shooting range with my adopted brother the police officer and shot a Desert Eagle 50 Caliber and a Glock 9mm. I had my first threesome in the hot tube with Kaylan M. and her best friend. I read *"The Art of Seduction"* by Robert Greene from Los Angeles. The book is popular in Hollywood. My older cousin Kimberly Phenicie told me about it. In 2002 and 2004 we were STATE CHAMPION Football Players. I put on an epic Defense in the state championship game Senior year and the other teams quarterback could hardly throw the ball. We creamed our opponents 38-0. The coach thanked me after the game. I was never as dedicated to academics as I could have been. I always expected to be an entrepreneur. I never expected to in any way rely on grades for success. Most of Hollywood has rebelled against formal schooling in one way or another. Nonetheless my physics teacher Stephen Wolfe told my parents I was the best student he ever had. I did Ace Physics twice, Art, Earth Science, Geometry, Physical Education four times, Physical Science, World Geography, Adobe Graphics, Senior Literature, Algebra II twice, U.S. History twice, Spanish I and Government/Economics. I also got an A in a Mountain Biking Class twice and convincing the school board to order supplies to build a freestyle bike park which I managed. I drew inspiration from films Like *World Disorder IV Ride The Lightening* (2003) and *Kranked V In Concert* (2003). I bought a Devinci 8-flat-8 Mountain bike and later bought a Marzocchi 888 RC. I was an Honor student Junior year. I had all As and a B like George Clooney. I wrote a paper titled "*Risk Assessment*" that my English teacher Todd Conaway published on the internet. At graduation that year Chris Gillespie and I staged a fight and he pretended to get knocked out after I faked a hard right cross. We had everybody going and Gillespie had to tell em it was a joke. I dated all the best looking girls in high school including both prom queens, Melissa Alexander, Jenny Parker, Annie Celina Bonaventure and Leonna Joy Kommer. There is a lot of love making in the Holy Bible, See Genesis 4, 4:17 and 4:25. During my Senior year I left every weekend because I was an adult. I remember staying at our quarterback Dane Ulett's house in Glendale and his mom passed out $100 bills to everyone before she left for New Jersey. My girlfriend senior year was already attending college in Tucson where I traveled on weekends. I moved down there for the spring semester in 2005 after graduation, where I lived with five girls. I went everywhere with my girlfriend Leonna Joy Kommer and her best friend Kirsten Miller. We lived at the Ranch at Star Pass with mostly other college students. At that time, the complex was new and had a swimming pool, gym, volley ball and tennis courts. It was a paradise. Leonna Joy Kommer happen to know Sunshine Johns from Seattle where Sunshine had lived until high school. I Met Joy in Arizona and I met Sunshine in Indiana. That happens all the time on Facebook. It's a small world. We also went to Mexico on the weekends. Kirsten's brother Jason Miller who was an off-road 4x4 enthusiast, introduced me to the sport. I graduated a semester early as I opted to attend summer school. I saw Gene Simmons at the Airport in Tucson. That summer my girlfriend and I worked in Alaska at a Lodge on Prince of Whales Island.

In the fall of 2005 I enrolled in Colorado Mountain College, Steamboat Springs with two of the girls I had dated in high school, Leonna Joy Kommer and Jenny Parker. Freshman year we all lived in the coed College Dorms before renting an apartment sophomore year. Some of my colleagues were Daniel Gunderson, Niall McNeice, Graham Owen, Jack McMullin and Didzis Bremze. During the summers I worked as a fly fishing guide for Bucking Rainbow Outfitters. During the winter I delivered pizza and hit the Mountains snowboarding at least five days a week and was doing back flips and 360s by the end of the first season. Steamboat is known for their world class Champagne Powder and their natural hot springs. At night clothing was optional. The Holy Bible says "Adam and his wife were both naked, and they felt no shame", See Genesis 2:25. I bought a black 2004 Nissan Frontier Crew Cab 6 speed manual 4x4 and lifted it. I bought oversize 285/70 R17 (33") BFG All-Terrains tires. I put a Shrockworks steel bumper on front with Hella

Lights and steel skid plates underneath. I used to drive to Moab, Utah to go off-roading and mountain biking. I hit Hell's Revenge and a few other trails. Once, I traveled with a Nissan group of about twenty vehicles from and online forum. We would talk on radios and walkie talkies while four wheeling. During the spring semester of 2007 I lived in Silverthorne, CO near Breckenridge in a house with Ian Bouchier, Ian Walker and Kieth Gerdes. I Boxed Gerdes who is 6'6" athletic build and I Won. I boxed Walker and Won after landing a spinning back fist. Bouchier didn't even want to Box after that. During the summer the lifts were open for hiking and Downhill Mountain biking. Freshman year I studied Martial Arts, Hapkido, Survey of Algebra, Mountain Biking, General Psychology, Physics I, Physics II, Batik II, Fly Fishing, College Algebra and Public Speaking. I Aced Survey of Algebra, Martial Arts, Mountain Biking and Fly Fishing Freshman year. After freshman year I started going to school part time mostly because I found working more interesting and I preferred working on social skills. Life for me is about diligence in any of the Professions I practice. I later studied Intro to PC Applications, Intro to Business, Human Nutrition, Introduction to philosophy, Career Development, Abnormal Psychology, English Composition I, English Comp II, Medical Terminology and U.S. Government. I Aced Intro to PC Applications, Abnormal Psychology and English Comp II. In Career Development I got a B and remember taking a test that said I was inclined to sales and management. In 2006 for my 20th birthday I went sky diving with Leonna Joy Kommer and Kieth Gerdes over Denver.

In 2007 I attended Semester at Sea through University of Virginia for the fall semester. UVA was founded by our third and fourth Presidents Thomas Jefferson and James Madison. Our ship with approximately seven hundred best and brightest college students in the country including many of the IVY League schools, departed from Ensenada, Mexico. It was good to be an American traveling the World and on an American Ship. I flew into San Diego and saw Kristen Field and David Rich who was in Law school at the time, they were both living out there. Our trip around the globe began with a first destination of Honolulu, Hawaii the day after my 21st birthday. There we chose an expedition of our choice. I chose a party boat snorkeling trip on the reef and rented surfboards in the evening. I had sex with a girl named Amanda in the harbor against the wall before we got back on the ship. She said she was salutatorian. Donald Trump bragged to Billy Bush the host of Access Hollywood, "I don't even wait. And when you're a star, they let you do it, you can do anything... grab them by the pussy.", before he was elected President of The United States. I have spent many years living like a star in that regard. The Semester at Sea staff would pass out condoms and told us to have fun safely.

Our next stop way Tokyo, Japan, the largest city in The World with a population of almost 40 million in the greater metropolitan area. The city was incredibly clean. During the day we explored the city and way of life and by night we experienced the restaurants and night clubs. From there my neighbors from the ship Tara Green Jackson who I dated, Marina Ivlev and my roommate Ryan Scott traveled south to Osaka by train with some others including Ben Greenly, Shane Foster and Mee Ah. Osaka was one of my favorite cities with an excellent night life. We met André Lauren Benjamin the famous hip hop Artist walking down the sidewalk. We met up with the boat a few days later when it came to port.

The next destination was Shanghai, China, also one of the biggest cities in The World. I traveled with Tara Jackson and Marina Ivlev and on our first night we found the two biggest Nightclubs in the city. One of the girls accidentally knocked over a speaker while dancing on stage and we were detained by police for a shake down. They kept asking for money and so we requested a phone call then called the

U.S. Embassy. They informed the police that they needed to let us go and they did. Then they gave us a ride to the airport and I flew with the girls to Beijing to see The Wonder of The World The Great Wall of China. It makes a good story because the U.S. Government backed us up on the other side of the world. Our stay was before the 2008 summer Olympics and the city was clearly in development. We stayed in a brand new hotel and had one of the most luxurious rooms I've ever stayed in. We then flew to Hong Kong and met up with the rest of the ship when it came to port.

Upon arrival in Chennai, India, I and a small group of colleagues were invited to do a home stay with the locals. The first night we stayed with a family that had a son in college, we discussed philosophy for hours and later went out with a group of students our age. We went to the Zoo and I slapped a crocodile. The second night I stayed with two girls in a home who's patriarch was a leader of the Rotary Club. I got a hand job from one of the girls. We had a great home cooked dinner and went shopping the next morning before a rotary event. Our host insisted upon buying us textiles.

After India we traveled to Vietnam where we stayed for a few days in Ho Chi Minh City, previously known as Saigon. We explored the country and I rented a boat with Jason Mays and his girlfriend Carolyn so we could see some of the islands in the area. We visited a war memorial where I shot an AK47. We shopped the downtown marketplace. The food was great.

Our Next Venture was Thailand. The ship ported in Bangkok, the country's capitol. We visit The Historic Grand Palace and traveled to Phuket where we spent most of our time. The first night there I wrestled Dan St.John who was a College Rugby player and he injured his foot pretty bad and I helped him get to the hospital. We visited the Phi Phi Islands. I watched a competitive Muay Thai fight and ate dinner on the beach with Melissa Roy, Peter West Neils and Alex Albarracin. Peter West Neils and I met two hot Thai girls. We took them back to the house they had rented and had sex with them on the Master bed. It was my first time fucking a girl with fake tits.

The ship then sailed to Alexandria, Egypt where we drove to Cairo, the largest city in Africa. I traveled with Ryan Nadeau, Alex Albarracin and a few others. We saw the Great Pyramids and paid $10 each for Camels all day. Before leaving we spent the day on a party dive boat exploring the ancient underwater city of Alexandria.

From Africa, we headed to Istanbul, Turkey, the Largest City in Europe. The City is built around the Bosphorus Strait between The Black Sea and The Sea of Marmara and is located in Europe and Asia. It is the only Metropolis in the world that exists on two continents on either side of the strait. After going to a Hookah Lounge we experienced one of the city's bath houses. That afternoon we visited the Istanbul University.

My final stop was Dubrovnik, Croatia where I was expelled from the ship along with a number of other students for drinking alcohol despite being 21 years of age. The city is one the most prominent tourist attractions on The Mediterranean Sea and has history dating back to the Seventh Century. We visited The Old Town stone walls and The Dubrovnik Castle before renting a hotel room where we had a little party and said our sayonaras before I caught my flight back to The U.S. the next morning.

On the ship I studied Philosophy, Sociology, Business and Macro Economics. I felt like a Celebrity all the way around the World. The U.S. Needs more Contemporary Architecture. I remember knowing I was much smarter than the Philosophy professor from the University of Virginia and the IVY League students. That was the first time someone told me I needed to write a Book. I have now been to twenty countries around the World which is more than most presidents. It was truly the best time of my life. It was a taste of a life style I must sustain. I'm pretty sure I dated more girls on that trip than anyone man. I usually traveled every country with a different group of people to make more connections. Tara Jackson said I was the most social person on the ship. I celebrated that 2008 New Years with my cousins in Chicago. We paid $120 cover each. I fingered three girls on the dance floor and another invited me to have sex with her in the bathroom. One of the girls had a guy with her and her friends. I put my fingers up to his nose so he could smell them and he did. He smelled my fingers and did a double take then seemed very interested in smelling my fingers again. The girls thought it was hilarious. I am Captain America.

CHAPTER 2

After the 2008 New Years I moved to Ft. Lauderdale, Florida a few blocks from Himmarshee St. It was a great place to move at the age of twenty one with with plenty of bars in the area and a lot of tourists having a good time. I used to approach the hottest girls I could find but that wasn't enough. I began dating off "Plenty of Fish" and sometimes had three dates per day. I had a very healthy dating life. There was a lot of talking and flirting going on. I slept with over one hundred women before I graduated college. Girls are fun. Nature is good. I donated blood and opted to be an organ donor on my Florida license. I also began training in Mixed Martial Arts and then Boxing. We would spar with groups of about twenty people. I would spar with everyone in the group. I was fast enough to hardly ever get hit, I'd either blocked punches or moved out of the way. I was Fast and erratic. Not even professional boxers could predict my moves. I was kicking a lot of ass fair and square and felt Superman. Between my new Dating Life and boxing I had a New sense of self, it was great. I was beating Pro Boxers and felt like I could do anything. This kind of Aptitude means I should be successful at anything I do. Pro boxers make $275 million per fight. I always thought I was supposed to be famous and this confirmed that I should be. A gym Owner and Coach who was an ex Pro Fighter also stated I was a "CHAMPION" after he saw me box a semi-pro fighter. I was Born in the Chinese Zodiac year of the Tiger. Someone said to me "If you are really cream of the crop you will rise to the top". Having a reputation that precedes is about women wanting to sleep with you before you meet them. In *Olympus Has Fallen* (2013) Aaron Eckhart portrayed a U.S. President as a Boxer. Vladimir Putin is a black belt in Judo and was a semi pro fighter before he was Elected president of Russia. Manny Pacquiao is now a Senator in the Philippines. It was also necessity at that time to know how to fight in South Florida. I got in two bar fights while I was there. One was in a Nightclub in Miami and a bunch of people got pushed out the door. Then someone pushed my wing man against the wall and started choking him. I pulled him off the guy off him and he came back at me so I hit him once in self-defense. Then that guy got pulled out of the Nightclub and the bouncers didn't say anything to me. Another time a guy was grabbing on my girl at Fat Cats in Ft. Lauderdale. I grabbed the guy by the neck with my right hand and took him to the ground then the bouncer pulled me off of him. I bought my U.S.A. Boxing license while living in Florida but never competitively fought. I did however spend a lot of time training to competitively fight. I found Boxing for me a little bit amoral beyond practical purposes and I didn't want to fight amateur fights that didn't pay. I also wasn't comfortable with anyone telling me who to fight. I remember the guy who arranged the fights said "Yeah... I'll get you fight" and said it like it would be a great injustice for me to fight. I got the feeling I was too good to fight! I figured I should be some where talking to people about helping the World. At some point I no longer came across anyone that was a threat. The best fighters don't start fights. I was in South Beach one day and I parked on the rooftop parking lot of an adult toy store. When I got back to my truck from the Beach there was a couple getting it on. I somehow talked my way into getting a hand job from this gorgeous woman while I rubbed her tits and he did her from behind. When we were done he said "Welcome to South Florida". I have met a lot of men who liked to give their wives whatever they wanted and would let me sleep with them. I went to Tarpon Bend, America's Backyard, Capones and all the other bars on Himmarshee. I like to dance with the girls. Dancing is also about making girls want to fuck and having a good time. I began bar tending with "MODEL BARTENDERS, INC." and promoting clubs in South Beach where I ran into people from Semester at Sea on two occasions. South Beach is a topless beach very sexy. Once I worked as a Bartender at a Party in North Miami Beach and I got a Blow job from the Birthday girl in front of a few other people. People used to invite me to Parties because they liked my Facebook page. I attended South Beach Bar Tending School in 2008 for fun. I worked at Ultra Music Festival as a bartender and at the Miami Heat Games in the American Airlines Arena as a VIP host. Both involved working in front of tens of thousands of people. I attended the 2008 "LANGERADO" music festival with my cousin Philip Boyd, Steven Paul and some others. I met up with some friends from Semester at Sea.

Then we went to a Victoria Secret's Pool Party in Miami where we saw Adriana Lima. I began working on TV sets in Miami as an Extra and knew Film and Television was what I needed to do. Darlene Gilbertie, the director at "One Source Talent" in Miami said my "Personality" was my strength and that I was the "NEXT BIG THING". A casting director in Miami stated I was "DEFINETLY A STAR". Then one day on set we were walking through the city to location and met a famous NBA player. We all took pictures with him and I remember a man telling me I was the "STAR". I work on "Burn Notice" for U.S.A. a number of times where I worked with Gabrielle Anwar and Jefferey Donovan. I was on *Confessions of a Shopaholic* (2009). I worked on Latin soap operas for Telemundo like "Mas Sabe el Diablo". I am naturally uninhibited and intelligent therefore I make a great Actor. When I started leaving set with the best looking girls there I figured it was meant for me. I had sex with a Canadian girl in my truck and she said my dick big. I went fishing with Ken Hinsley who was a Kicker in the NFL. We went kite fishing for Sailfish on his boat off Miami and the fishing was better than expected. I started dating a girl named Olivia B. and her best friend Jennifer who was in Law School and who I had met at a line dancing bar called the "Roundup" in Davie, FL. Jennifer came up to me and said "Hey come talk to my friend" and that's how we all met. Olivia worked at a Tanning Salon and got us into the Hard Rock Casino Night Clubs for free where we also drank for free, so we went there almost every weekend. We also got free tans. I bought a bright blue Toyota Tacoma TRD Off-Road King Cab 6 speed manual 4x4 and lifted it myself on Donahoe adjustable Coil-overs and Icon Vehicle Dynamics leaf springs with remote reservoir shocks. I put it on oversize 265/75 R16 (31.6") BFG All-Terrain tires. On Halloween I got in a fight with a guy hitting on my girl. I was a Boxer for Halloween wearing robe with gloves strapped to the outside of wrists and a drink in hand. I said to him "maybe I should have brought two pairs of gloves" because boxing is a sport that requires two pairs of gloves I said I didn't have. Instead of him saying "Oh excuse me, I know this is your girlfriend, I was just leaving" or simply denying any intentions to want to fight he said "I'll fight you bare knuckles in the backyard right now". I had fight bite on my right hand from defending my friend in that Night club in Miami. My right hand was swollen and useless I wasn't at all serious about Boxing but the way he reacted it was clear he thought he could kick my ass and take my girl. I obviously wasn't going to back down. We went outside. He swung first then we started wrestling because I couldn't couldn't punch him with my hand swollen. I broke the guys jaw with my knee in Self-Defense after he tried to gouge my eye, See Rowe v. U.S., 164 U.S. 546 (1896). I went inside. When he walked in the house his jaw sticking out the side of his face and he couldn't talk. Then Jennifer in law school pulled me into a room and got on her knees and attempted to suck my Dick but strings on my board shorts turned into a knot. After a moment or two of frustration she gave up. My girlfriend was in the next room and the door was open. I realized afterwards that South Florida Code of Conduct requires that you do your girl's best friend. One of the girls recorded the fight on her phone and we could hear the guys jaw snap. It was the most brutal fight I've ever been in. The moral of the story is don't fight don't start fights and I don't like to fight. The beauty of the second amendment is people treat each other with respect because they they know disrespect could lead to someone getting shot. Firearms require citizens to think carefully about how to handle themselves and deal with confrontation. I took a full time job as a para-transit operator for a company named "Village Car Service". I enjoyed the Public Service helping the elderly and handicap to and from wherever they needed to go. The job was very hands on I would lift the passengers and help them in and out of the vehicle and to and from their homes. I used a hydrophilic lift on the back of the van to get passengers in wheel chairs on board then would buckle them in so they they could travel safely. There is a link to a video about the job on my website. I drove an F-250 with a V10. The CEO called me the "Good Guy" because I often got multiple call in compliments each day. I was still going to school part time and working Seventy Hour per weeks. Often working fourteen hour days and didn't mind. This lasted for about a year. The company was unfortunately under bid by a competitor from NY and we lost our contract with the state. Village Car Service was shut down. My roommate in South Florida was Galloway Selby. He was a shipyard Director and before that he managed a resort in Costa Rica. His son Keegan Ray Selby trades cryptocurrencies from Los Angeles and is a Co-Founder of Fourth Revolution Capitol. He also became a good friend. He is on Youtube. When I could I spent time surfing, fishing, playing volleyball and football on the beach and free diving. I bought a kayak and used to spend up to six hours at a time on the ocean spearfishing and hunting lobster to eat. It helped me stay in shape. I used to be able to hold my breath up to five minutes and dive 100 ft. I also met up with some of my good friends from middle school including Daniel Barton and Carolyn Fortson who I went Wake boarding with on weekends. I went fishing and diving with Tim Maguire and Terry Durante. I Bought a hand gun that shoots shotgun shells called a Taurus Judge Magnum 45 Colt/410 Mag that was in the Movie *Max Payne* (2008). I went jet skiing and to House parties with Cyrus Mousavi and Diana Szabo who lived near me and who I had met at a night club. While in Florida I studied Art Appreciation, Music Appreciation, English II and Ethics before graduating in 2010 with an Associate of Arts from Colorado Mountain College. Twelve Presidents didn't even graduate college. Truman didn't go to college until thirty nine. Mark Zuckerberg and Bill Gates both dropped out of college after two years. No matter what you do If you plan to rise to the top and help the world and I always have you must speak on TV. I decided to move to Hollywood to Act Professionally.

In May of 2010 I moved to California for Film and Television. Along the way I saw Kieth Gerdes in Breckenridge, Colorado where I bought a beautiful Winchester 12 Gauge Pump Wood Stock and went Trap Shooting in Reno, NV. I saw my roommate from Semester at Sea Ryan Scott who lived in San Francisco. We stayed at his family house on Lake Tahoe. During the day we went snowboarding and that night we had a party with girls we had met. We both had sex with girls. After a night in Tahoe and a night in San Francisco I stayed with an Asian girl I had dated on Semester at Sea named Sherrie Mi in San Jose who worked at Google. From there I continued my journey south and drove to San Diego where I unloaded my truck into storage. I then returned to Los Angeles for entertainment and stayed with my roommate from La Lumiere James Comstock and his girlfriend in Woodland Hills with their roommate who was a bank teller. I applied to the LAPD (Los Angeles Police Department) and passed the written and physical tests but they didn't offer me anything. I got the impression it was because they thought I was too straight. They recommended I look into CHP(California Highway Patrol) who also do not require a college degree although I had one and their website states they prefer applicants who do have a degree but I never did. My adopted half brother had also suggested I apply to state police in Florida after he became a police officer but I of course wanted to live in California. I applied to the San Diego Sheriff's Department because I had no idea they required deputies to work in jail for a year. I saw that the San Fransisco Police Department paid $100,000 a year but I didn't apply because I wanted to make connections in Los Angeles and Hollywood. I planned to quit after a year or two anyways like Eddie Money, Chuck Norris, Erik Estrada, Shaquille O'Neal, Dean Cain, Dan Aykroyd, David Zayas, Dennis Farina, Steve Wilkos, Ted Nugent, J.W. Cortez and Elvis Presley. I met a girl at a gym in

Malibu and we had sex in the back seat of my Tacoma which isn't usually considered illegal if people can't see and I had tinted windows. She said she used to date Brad Garrett from "Everybody Loves Raymond". I met Kiefer Sutherland the Actor in Malibu while having breakfast at an Irish roadhouse. I noticed him when I sat down. He came over and shook my hand while I was at my table. I also saw Tim Allen at Starbucks in Studio City. I saw Kevin Hart the comedian at the Warner Center in Woodland Hills. I gave a ride to a girl in Topanga Canyon when her Jaguar broke down. She had to leave but invited me to stay at her house while she was out of town. I went to Ryan Berkowitz Birthday Pool Party at the "Viceroy" in Santa Monica. I took a summer job as a sales representative at LA Fitness in Downtown Hollywood. The gym was located in a remodeled Movie theater on the Hollywood strip and it's members worked in the entertainment industry. It was an atmosphere I wanted to be in and a good place to network. I liked to ask everyone what they did for a living. At that time the job consisted of corporate sales, sales, promotions, and giving tours of the gym. I enjoyed working for commission. I spent half of my time doing promotions and giving away free two week gym passes around the City and at Runyon Canyon where I met Keith David the Actor. I met Michael C. Hall from the TV show "Dexter" at Ralph's in Hollywood. I would invite prospective members to use the gym for a free trial then sell them a membership after. It was an excuse to talk to hundreds of Californians each day. The passes had a value of over $200 and I like giving away free stuff. I spent about a month working in Hollywood and then transferred to the Universal City location where I made more money. I met an beautiful black Actress and Singer named Rayietta "Kodi" Hill at the Universal City gym and we were inseparable for about a month. She has an IMDB. I later found out she was married but her white stock broker husband didn't seem to mind. We basically walked into each other when we met. I took lunch and walked out of the gym with her under my arm. She showed me around the city and introduced me to her friends. We spend time meeting producers and going to recording studios. We used to go to the Nightclubs and I would pretend I knew the bouncers or they would pretend to know me and we would walk right in and cut the line. She drove a Blue BMW X5. One day while we were driving to Santa Monica from the valley on the 405 a sudden traffic jam caused the vehicles to stop. The driver behind me wasn't paying attention and hit the back of my vehicle. We took pictures and video and opted not to involve the police even though he was driving without insurance. The driver got out and gave me a hug and said he was glad we were okay and that he was sorry. I took pictures of his drivers license and of the vehicles and sent it to my insurance company. The estimator declared the vehicle totaled because the frame was bent in front of the rear bumper. State Farm settled with me for almost $20,000 which was more than I paid for the vehicle. I considered buying a Nissan 350z and took a few test drives but ended up buying my truck back from State Farm for $5,000 because it still drove perfectly. I decided to use the money to invest in my acting career. I paid $300 for acting photos from MICHAEL ROUD to get me started and quit my job at LA Fitness. I spoke with Melissa Roy from Semester at Sea and she recommended Mike Pointer for an acting coach. I attended as many acting classes as I could across LA including Jen and Paolo Krater, Sal Landi, Chris Berube, Jake Carpenter, Bruce Hickey and Kirk Baltz. Acting is about self Mastery. All the acting coaches were giving me the thumbs up, they said I had it. I also studied acting in a theater in Hollywood where I would perform on stage before a crowd of people every week. Boxing became a fallback. I knew I could have started fighting at any time to get on TV which would have likely led to other opportunities as it did for Mickey Rourke. On Halloween I met a Model named Kristin F. who I had sex with in the restroom of the bar on Abbot Kinney Blvd in

Venice. She told me my Dick was big. My First principle role was on America's Court with Judge Kevin Ross. I played a defendant in an episode titled "Where's my Scooter". I met judge Alex Ferrer in Hollywood while working audience on his show. He came down afterwards and I got to talk to him. I also worked audience for Judge Joe Brown. I printed comp cards with my new photos and sent them to Talent Agencies in Los Angeles. I got three interviews from my pictures. The first agent offered me a contract and I said I would take it home and read it and then bring it back to him. For whatever reason he had a problem with me taking a copy of the contract and reading over it before making a decision. Maybe he didn't understand I had two other meetings. Then I met "ONE STAR TALENT AGENCY" who not only offered me representation they offered me an internship as an agent. I spent a few hours a day submitting myself and the other actors for auditions. "Casting Networks" and "Actors Access" were the two main platforms that allow actors with their completed profiles to submit to castings. They do allow actors to personally submit to castings however Agents and Managers have access to higher paying jobs that aren't available to those without representation. I also registered with "Central Casting" for Extra work. The Daniel Hoff Agency used to hold auditions for representation once a week. I went there and got a call back. I worked on *Life Happens* (2011) directed by Kat Coiro. We Filmed in a Nightclub in Hollywood. At that time the Film was titled "BFF & Baby". Kristen Johnston called all the girls on set "sluts". Then one of the Extras grabbed my ass and tried to do me in her car. I worked on CSI: NY as an Extra and then was upgraded to a stand-in. My career began to build momentum and I was booking more auditions, filling up my resume and expanding my portfolios. I was getting green lights. I met Flo-Rida the rapper at Runyon Canyon where I saw Johnny Knoxville and the Game. I asked Flo-Rida if he played in the NFL because I didn't recognize him. He said he did Music and gave me a fist pound pound while getting in his car. Within a few months I was in an ESPN SUPER BOWL COMMERCIAL that I saw play on TV during the 2011 Championship. It was one of the most viewed programs in World History. I was working as an Extra however they put me and a hot girl in the last scene center of camera. My date and I walked away from a Fair as it blew up behind us like a scene from a Hollywood Action Movie. I was a Party Goer in *For The Love of Money* (2012) with Director Ellie Kanner and I met Inbar Lavi and Delphine Chanéac. Inbar Lavi said acting was like "lying" but I disagree. It's more like story telling. I was a Club Patron in *Sugar* (2013) and I met Shenae Grimes-Beech and she told me she was on the New 90210. I met John O'Hurley in studio City. He was the Host of "Family Feud". In 2010 I attended EDC the Electronic Daisy Carnival in Los Angeles. In late 2010 I sublet a studio apartment at the Asbury in downtown Los Angeles off 6th St. and Alvarado then I moved to Korea town and lived with Sanyika Street a 6'8" 280 lb African-American musician and actor who is on Youtube. I liked Korea town and used to play football in front of the apartments with the teenagers in the neighborhood. I often spent three to four hours a day in the gym because I want to live like a rock star. I had a nice six pack. The feeling of being in such Elite physical condition is Superhuman. I was already a great Boxer and now I was in astronomically better shape. My Stamina was phenomenal. I did an hour of cardio in the morning before the sun came up and and a few hours of weights in the afternoon every day. I began to study Movement and take dance lessons at "Millennium", the "Edge" and other studios across the City. I practiced Hip hop, Line Dancing, Bachata, Break Dancing and Salsa. I met Oscar Nominee Nare Mkrtchyan dancing at a Nightclub in Santa Monica. She has an IMDB. The best thing I ever did to improve my ability as a fighter was Dance. I once went to a professional Dance audition in North Hollywood. I didn't know it was a Dance audition until I got there.

I tried out and lasted ten minutes. I was in a Hyundai Commercial that shot for two days on a San Bernardino racetrack and paid $300 per day. I booked a Corbis photo shoot in Malibu that paid $300 titled "Love". I worked with Photographer Drew Myers. I was cast as a Naval Captain in a Scientology film with Golden Era Productions that shot at their movie production center in San Jacinto. I wore a fake porn star mustache and has my shirt off in the Movie titled History of L. Ron Hubbard. I met Alison Eastwood and worked with Clint Eastwood and Leonardo Dicaprio on "J. Edgar". I was on the set twice at the Warner Brother's Studios in Burbank. Most of Hollywood at one time worked for background rates when they were first getting into the industry. I remember working on set and Dicaprio came over riding a bicycle. He pretended he was having a hard time riding the bicycle and keeping his balance and made me laugh. I was on that set twice. The last time I was on set was the night before I flew to New York. I eventually signed with "MIDWEST TALENT" and then "L&L TALENT" in Los Angeles. I also had a manager named Jacqueline Kennedy from "BREAK-A-LEG TALENT AGENCY". I booked my first casting with them, a "CARTIER" watch print job that shot at a private airport. I was on a BMW motorcycle wearing a Cartier watch in front of my private Jet. The job paid $400. I was on a VH1 show called "YOU'RE CUT OFF" in the seventh episode "Alone On The Range". I was an EMT on "1000 WAYS TO DIE" Directed by Alex Harvey. I was on *Scorned* (2013) Directed and written by Mark Jones and by Sadie Katz. I had met a number of people from NYC while working in the industry, including a Manhattan Club promoter and Actor that I liked so I decided to fly out there and get agent.

On March 1st 2011 I flew to NYC and rented car, then I found an apartment Brooklyn. I lived with a doctor in residency. I prefer Los Angeles but I do like how many people are in Manhattan. Since when did it become normal for people to not like other people? I mailed out comp cards to agents and was soon signed with "EXPECTING MODELS", "PLAZA 7 TALENT AGENCY", "ROSS TALENT AGENCY", "D2 MODELS" and another Agency I can't remember the name of. Talent agencies weren't exclusive like they were on the west coast. An actor or model is free to be represented by as many agencies as he or she likes, whoever presents the opportunity first gets the commission. I just tell them when I'm in the city and ready to work. On the west coast an actor may only have one talent agent for Film and Television, another for Commercial and Print and one manager, and actors are bound by contracts. Agents and managers usually take about twenty percent if they get you the audition and you book the job. Very successful entertainers have better contracts and pay less in agent and manager fees. I stayed very busy for the month I was in NY and worked about five days per week and if I wasn't working I would be meeting with production companies through castings. By April my resume was off the page. I did an Internship at "IMPOSSIBLE CASTING" and then booked my very next audition there, a "YAHOO Genome" Internet commercial that paid $400. I did a photo shoot in Queens with a photographer for his college graduation project. We had two girls to hold reflectors and do wardrobe. It was a great shoot and some of my best pictures. My second week in New York I was working on the set of "New Years Eve" in Times Square where I met a girl named Raquel Toro who has an IMDB. On set I also worked with Ryan Seacrest, Ashton Kutcher, Michael Bloomberg and Director Gary Marshall. Mayor Bloomberg tried to shake my hand. I was on the set two days in a row. Raquel and I dated for the next two weeks I was there and before I left she invited me to stay with her in her upper east side apartment when I returned.

I flew back to Los Angeles in April 2011 and with resume credits off the page and I booked more work then before. I was in a "XOOM.COM" BBC National commercial that shot in Santa Monica and Burbank and paid $800. At the Audition in Los Angeles I was a man cheering for a sports team. I remember the Producer saying he was impressed with my new resume because he had seen me once before and I didn't have many credits when I first started. I got the job. I was in "FARMER BOYS" local Southern California commercial with "LYON STUDIOS" that paid $600. I had to drive all the way to Orange County for the Audition. I played Aqua Man in a National Commercial for "DC NATION" that paid $400. It was filmed partially in the Long Beach Aquarium and I got to swim in the tank. I was Cast in a "FRANCE 2" TV Promo with "PARADOXAL" Productions that paid $200. I was very busy during this time. I remember having three auditions in a day. It's a measure of success to get invited to auditions and I got a lot of them. I also booked a photo shoot for "BODYMAKER" a Japanese clothing Company that paid $600. I met a girl at a hotel swimming pool party in Los Angeles and had sex with her, she said the sex was so good I "ruined" her life. Honestly, I never meant to ruin anyone's life. Once I had a commercial reel put together, I not only booked better work as I appeared to be a more established Actor but larger Talent agencies including IDIOM and CESD began writing me and offering me representation.

In May of 2011 I flew back to Manhattan. I booked my first Audition through Plaza 7 Talent for a $2,500 photo shoot. I booked several more shoots that summer through Expecting Models for jobs ranging from $1,100 to $1,250. One of which was for "ANVIL" Sportswear. I was making over 200% what the President of The United States makes per day at the age of twenty four as an Independent Contractor in Marketing and Entertainment. I walked up and down Manhattan like I owned the place and no one had a problem with it. I enjoyed every second of it. I thought I should be making millions but you have to start somewhere. I played a Husband in a "PANASONIC" Commercial with "ZAZOU PRODUCTIONS". I was also cast for a stock photography shoot for "GETTY IMAGES" that shot in upstate New York and paid $800. Ashling Schiffelbian came to visit me while I rented an apartment in Brooklyn for a month. When I heard the Screen Actors Guild and the American Federation of Television and Radio Artists unions were going to merge, I decided to join AFTRA to get into SAG-AFTRA. I paid $1,500 to get into the union and after the merge the initiation fee went up to $3,000. Union members are required to pay dues twice a year however generally get paid more for their time than non-union entertainers. For extra work which is fairly easy to get the day base rate is $168 per day or $21 per hour for eight hours. The commercial extra rate was $300 per day. Sometimes they let wrap early and we still got paid the full day rate. Sometimes we worked overtime for for time and a half. I made about $30,000 my first year between Principal and background work. I saw Dr. Oz and Nikki Menage in Manhattan that summer. I took an acting class in a theater in Manhattan where I did a monologue from the movie "Wall Street" on stage in front of a crowd. The scene was from Michael Douglas giving a speech to Wall Street traders. I bought a Cannon 60D DSLR camera and other equipment. I bought two lavalier microphones, two Zoom H1n audio recorders, an External Flash, two Contour high definition sports cameras, a SLIK tripod and mono pod and later a studio setup with green screen and lights. I had worked with enough Directors and Photographers that I wanted to have a go at it. I not only intended to use the camera for photography the Cannon DSLRs are great for cinematography, See *Black Swan* (2010). I knew at the very least the camera would come in handy for me to expand my portfolios, record auditions and make demo reels. I thought it would be a great way to make money. I spent a lot of time learning to use computer professional programs like Photo Shop, Logic, Soundtrack Pro and Final Cut Pro X. I Aced PC Applications in College and Adobe Graphics in High school the only two computer courses I ever took. I also loaded Enhancement software onto the camera's computer call "Magic Lantern" that has a lot of additional features. Raquel Toro worked at "Hachette" Book Group and had a free subscription to Lynda.com which gives video tutorials on many of these programs. I learned award winning films making over $100 million were being made with the new High Definition Cannon DSLRs. I was eager to start Filming. I filmed a Kaplan College Hosting Demo where I walked towards the camera talking in a sports park in Los Angeles. Most of the work I was getting didn't have lines and I needed a Demo of me speaking to the camera viewers. I looked like I could run for governor at twenty four. I want deals like Ryan Seacrest who makes over $75 million per year because I am good at it. I also made a couple short films about trap shooting and fishing. I Filmed a short titled "Celebrating Second Amendment Rights in America" where I threw multiple clay pigeons in the air and shot them before they hit the ground. I dubbed "Enter Sandman" by Metallica on some great video and was happy with it. I didn't study law or politics at the time or my inclination may have been to make a Film about that. However, one can make quite the artistic creation without dialogue and I was having fun learning to use the camera. The next Short Film I made was a commercial for my guide service of summer steelhead fishing in the Midwest. I used "Thanks for The Pepperoni" by George Harrison with the edited and color corrected footage and thought it came out great. In August I decided to take a road trip down Baja to make a Documentary about fishing for Roosterfish from 4X4s on the Beaches. I love to feel like a rich white man in Mexico. I called producer Todd Moen and asked him if he would like to go with me. He said he couldn't. I flew back to California then drove down to San Diego and went to REI to get some more supplies before my trip. I filmed everything from the boarder crossing to fishing, diving and driving and named the Film "Baja Adventure" which later went to the

Film Festivals and is now on my IMDB. I drove all the way to Cabo San Lucas where I had sex with three American girls in one day. I met a girl named Danette Reid on "Model Mayhem" and did a photo shoot. She invited me to stay at her house while she went to "Burning Man". I spent three weeks in Mexico. I also bought two prime lenses that summer for portraiture as I heard they were the best. I started a portfolio of actors and models and built a photography business. I help Actors and Models look their best and get their careers started. I am CEO of "TAEBEL PHOTOGRAPHY". I charge $300 for two to three looks. A Fashion Photographer by the name of Alberto Diaz Gutierrez helped young Doctor Ernesto "Che" Guevara and Guerrilla Leader Fidel Castro overthrow the Cuban government, See *CHEVOLUTION* (2008). Many of my clients sign release waivers for reduced rates therefore I can use the photos in stock photography portfolios with Corbis and Getty Images.

CHAPTER 3

In late August I returned to New York. Raquel and I rented a cabin on the Delaware River for the weekend to celebrate my 25th birthday that week. The day before my birthday I had an unusual encounter with the building bellhop. He hassled me about a permission slip and spoke to me in a tone that gave me the impression he thought he could kick my ass. The bellhop was 6'3" and 301 lbs named Frank Martoni. I don't like to be talked down to by guys his size or by my own bellhop. I text Raquel about it and said if that guy touches me I'll "beat his ass". I was a trained martial artist and boxer and felt like a lethal weapon but I had restraint and was very much aware that he would have to threaten me first with unlawful force before an ass kicking would be legal. There is nothing wrong with being aggressive when a man plays by the rules. That would be like telling a professional Athlete they are playing too competitively or too passionately. Life in many ways is like a sports game with rules and when someone plays by the rules no one can tell them they are playing too aggressive. I have a right to feel comfortable on the property of my residence and being harassed and then assaulted by a bellhop was unacceptable. The behavior warranted an ass whooping legally and ethically. I had taken two semesters of self-defense in college. In a formal educational setting we learn to respect the lawful use of force, the law and other people's rights. NY Penal Law § 35.15 states: "...a person may use physical force upon another individual when, and to the extent that, he/she reasonably believes it to be necessary to defend himself/herself [or someone else] from what he/she reasonably believes to be the use or imminent use of [unlawful] physical force by such individual." Opposition to stand your ground law doesn't discourage crime it leads to unjustified prosecutions. If someone doesn't like getting their ass whooped then they shouldn't assault people in the first place. The "Roommate Law" Real Property Law § 235-f states in section (3) that that any person who enters into a lease agreement by themselves has the right to an additional "occupant" and Section (5) states that person can move in without first notifying building management. The New York City Administrative Code § 26-521 states it is unlawful to attempt to evict someone who has lived in a residence for "30 days" or longer without a warrant of eviction. This is a standard law across the country, in many states its much less than 30 days. I knew this because I had previously had this very discussion over dinner with my adopted brother Ryan Taebel who was a detective in Gainesville, FL. I knew the bellhop, regardless of his insolence, could not use physical force to prevent me from entering the building and accessing my apartment. The apartment had been my primary residence since May and I had been staying there every night since March, almost six months prior. The Supreme Court of The United States ruled self-defense isn't just about protecting one's self physically but is about defending one's legal rights, See Brown v. U.S., 256 U.S. 335 (1921). I clearly had a legal right to access my apartment. I wasn't going to back down to a threat on my own property and legally I didn't have to. We just had a President Elected who wrote "I was a pretty tough kid. I wanted to be the toughest kid in the neighborhood and had a habit of mouthing off to everyone and backing down to no one... I wasn't afraid to fight...", see *Great Again: How to Fix Our Crippled America*" by Donald J. Trump the Book he published while Campaigning for President. Never back down. The bellhop was trying to be a dick and got what he deserved. One would think a doorman should have a little more respect for a resident who had lived in the building for almost six months. I like helping people like I did in college and I will be happy to when I have the resources. This is about a Doorman who was way out of line. He started it and escalated it. I was just going to my apartment and that is my absolute right. Jesus couldn't possibly be more justified than just going to his dwelling, See Rowe v. U.S., 164 U.S. 546 (1896). The Supreme Court ruled where the assailant was killed "it was error to make the case depend, in whole or in part, upon the inquiry whether the accused could, by stepping aside, have avoided the attack, or could have so carefully aimed his pistol as to paralyze the arm of his assailant, without more seriously wounding him.", See Rowe v. U.S., 164 U.S. 546 (1896). This essentially means that someone who is attacked may objectively use all necessary force to stop an attack, as I did. I walked out of the building for coffee passing the bellhop who saw me. When I returned a short while later he again hassled me about permission to enter, I had been seeing this guy almost every day for six months, I said I lived in the building and kept walking. Then the manager who I had met once before said something and I turned to her and shook her hand and said again "I Live in the building" then I proceeded to the elevator. The bell hop aggressively started following me and when the elevator door opened he physically tried to stop me. I pushed back and slammed him into the back wall then let him go so he would leave but he didn't leave he attacked me again, this time hitting me in the face. I wasn't going to hit the guy unless he hit me first. I gave him a right hook just hard enough to repel the attack. He was stunned and didn't want any more. He got his balance back after leaning against the wall for a few seconds then he walked out of the elevator. It was a textbook perfect self-defense, he had hit me first and there was lobby video of this guy using unlawful force to stop me when the law clearly states without a warrant for eviction he shouldn't have been trying to stop me in the first place. This case is so obviously self-defense anyone with at least an elementary IQ should agree. I was well within my legal rights. Self-defense law particularly favors a person on property of their residence however I was unlawfully arrested by confused police who had spoke to the bellhop and who clearly had no idea what they were doing. I was on my own property of residence, The Castle Doctrine applies. The arrest was for a misdemeanor without a warrant. I received a desk appearance ticket and was back to the building in a few minutes. I expected the courts would dismiss it. I expected people in a court room to be a lot smarter than the police or the bellhop however the courts refused to dismiss the charges or give me a probable cause hearing and they pushed for trial or a plea agreement. I had already represented myself in court in Los Angeles twice, once for driving on an allegedly suspended license for a California license I never applied for and another for a traffic violation. I was one hundred percent successful getting the allegations dismissed both times. I have personally seen that a single officers testimony of a traffic violation doesn't usually hold up in court if contested. I pushed for a dismissal because I didn't want an assault conviction, I wanted a concealed weapons permit and because I wanted to sue the Building Management company. They offered me probation for a misdemeanor but I declined. Things got really ugly when after nine months they secured fraudulent testimony before a grand jury and indicted me for Assault "with intent for serious injury" claiming they had come across new evidence and the injury was worse than previously recognized. After the law required the charges to be dismissed for speedy trial they indicted it to coerce a plea agreement, See NY Criminal Procedure Law § 30.30 that requires dismissal after six months. The building management company must have had a meeting with their lawyers about what happened and they realized they couldn't tell it like it happened or they would be at fault. The bellhop claimed he never intended to use physical force but the lobby cameras show hostile body language as he followed me out of camera view. He claimed he had been hit not once but "four times" in an unprovoked attack despite obvious video footage to the contrary. Nothing in the pictures, medical reports or police reports indicated he had been hit more than once in fact they all inferred he had been hit only once. In all the UFC fights I've ever watched I've never seen someone hit four times in the same spot, this is an implausible story on its face. A person tends to move or block after being hit once, if they get hit again, it's isn't in the same spot. The bellhop claimed he had suffered a fracture that required a permanent metal plate to be surgically implanted. I was 5'11" about 175 lbs at that time, the bellhops medical reports said he was 6'3" 301 lbs, that's over 125 lbs bigger than I was. This is also implausible. That's like a light Heavy weight beating a Super Heavyweight with a single punch. The testimony I know was fraudulent and the medical reports probably were as well. Anyone could prove it was false evidence and he never had surgery or a metal plate put in his head with a metal detector. The injury however is almost entirely irrelevant from the primary issue of concern which is whether or not he had a right to use physical force in the first place which of course he did not and the video proves his intentions to use force before walking of camera and it proves he was the initial aggressor. The judge by the way did refer to him as a "bellhop". A respectable man usually holds in high regard the principals self-defense and laws of nature. That's why it never made sense for them to press the charges, they should have respected it as the text book perfect self-defense it was. Weeks later hundreds if not thousands of "Occupy Wall Street" protesters were illegally arrested in Manhattan where police made arrests with giant nets arresting large groups of people at a time. Most of the charges were dismissed and many sued and were awarded damages. Also see the malicious prosecution of Michael Premo for assault on an officer.

For the next sixteen months I continued to work as an Actor, Filmmaker and Photographer. I was building all my portfolios. And I was flying back to NYC from Los Angeles every month to go to Court appearances. I saw Anderson Cooper at the Manhattan Courthouse. He rode a bicycle to the Courthouse. I was in NYC for hurricane Sandy and could see cars mostly submerged under flood water out my second floor window. I took video and sent it to CNN. I booked my first principle SAG-AFTRA role in a Fantasy Football commercial that shot in a parking garage on the upper east side of Manhattan. I was originally booked as an extra however there was a casting and a call back before I was booked which is unusual for extra work. The role required me to drive a motorcycle next to a vehicle through a parking garage as if to escort the driver. The job was dangerous and I expected it to be for the stunt performer day rate of $630 however they intended to only pay the background rate. I spoke with the producers after the shoot and they wrote me a new contract as a principle performer. Raquel and I had a hearing in housing court and when I explained to the judge what happened he said "It looks like there is fault on both sides" which indicated that criminal charged couldn't lawfully be pressed. A month later the bellhop returned to work and said "good morning" to me but I just kept walking. I don't think he had surgery because the medical reports indicated he had surgery a few weeks after the incident and I saw him not long after that without any scar or bandage. I was in a "KIPLINGER" Magazine Editorial. I worked with Photographer "Allison Michael Orenstein". I had two stock photography shoots with "JLP STUDIOS" in NYC. I worked with Photographer Paul Aresu in a project titled "RINESCO". During this time after the arrest I met with a number of lawyers in Manhattan and Los Angeles and I was more competent than any of them. I met a doctor in residency off "Tinder" who lived in Brooklyn. She answered her door and we started kissing. She played a video of her having sex with two guys on her computer. Then we had sex. I was cast on "Fatal Attractions". I played a husband who came home to his hot wife. She dropped her robe when I came in the door and stood there in lingerie. I walked over and grab her and we started kissing. I was cast on "Celebrity Close Calls" and played officer "Betz" as listed on my IMDB. I was on MIB III the Movie and in the crowd of spectators during the shuttle launch scene in Florida. I saw Bono in NYC. I also booked an "ASTON LEATHER" Photo shoot modeling Leather jackets that cost thousands each. I worked with Adam Metin the President and Owner. I did a few internet advertisements. I was in an "INTERCLICK" Marketing Advertisement. I saw Mike Rowe in West Hollywood. I was an Athlete in a "SMB MARKETING GROUP" Video. And I was in a "PANASONIC" Video with CARBON PRODUCTIONS. I was on "BLUE BLOODS" which airs on CBS. I saw a girl in Manhattan one night that was passed out and wouldn't wake up even when she was being dropped on the pavement. I asked them if she had taken any pills with the alcohol and they said "yes". I said I thought she should go to the hospital and they said "okay". I left after EMTs got her. While I was walking home later that night I couldn't stop wondering if that girl was okay so I walked to the hospital and asked. After describing her and getting her first name correct the doctors took me to her said she was going to be fine. I was glad to see her smiling when she woke up. From October through November in 2012 I filmed "BEST OF FALL-Fishing Great Lake's Tributaries for Steelhead and Salmon" which later Won first place "Feature Film" from the "SWEET AS FILM FESTIVAL" in Toronto, Canada February 2017. When I was editing the Movie I had the house and property all to myself and when four of my neighbors climbed over the fence to play tennis in our back yard I ran out there and kicked them all out because I was making the movie. I obviously took the film very seriously and am glad it Won and Award. The Film is now listed on my IMDB. I made it Montauk that fall to surf cast for Stripers and Blue fish amongst the crowds. I did pretty well. I never felt one hundred percent while I had charges pending against me and the stress of the indictment was debilitating. My career fell off after I was arrested on the Upper East side of Manhattan and definitely after nine months later when it was indicted. It's hard enough to book auditions, everything has to feel right. I had to feel on top of my life to succeed in the industry and I didn't when I was being criminally prosecuted. The Supreme Court has ruled, "a defendant confined to jail prior to trial is obviously disadvantaged by delay as is a defendant released on bail but unable to lead a normal life because of community suspicion and his own anxiety.", See Barker v. Wingo, 407 U.S. 514 (1972).

In January of 2013 the case was set for trial. I think the building management company who was a regular campaign contributor had influence over the district attorney's office. They didn't want the charges dismissed because they didn't want to get sued or they were prosecuting me for not backing down. After I had stated I wanted to represent myself there was about thirty reporters outside the courthouse at my next appearance. I thought they were there for me but they were there to see Lindsay Lohan who also had court that day. A female judge at the 100 Centre St. Court House asked me what my pretrial motion was and I said "Motion To Dismiss" for speedy trial, however she transferred the case across the street to a homosexual judge who was a president of a gay and lesbian judge association. Because I couldn't get them to dismiss the charges I proceeded to trial. I made a the big mistake of not calling the Media which I would never do again. The judge denied the text message I intended to present as evidence for no valid reason at a pre-trial evidentiary hearing. The text stated "If that guy touches me I will beat his ass." The text was regarding the bellhop several days prior to the incident and proved that I acted in premeditated Self-Defense and that I had not lost my temper and acted irrationally or spontaneously. The guy looked like scum that didn't care if you lived or died. I asked the judge if I could make an audio recording of the trial and he refused to allow me to do that. I also threatened to call the ACLU and he said "what's the ACLU going to do?". I opted not to make any voir dire questions or peremptory challenges because I was conserving my energy and I thought the case should be simple enough for anyone to acquit me. I made a strong opening statement and insinuated the charges as a clearly malicious prosecution. Then the judge faked getting sick and the case was postponed for over a week. All the while I was spending a lot of money to stay in expensive Manhattan hotels. They didn't resume the trial until I felt exhausted. When the trial finally did continue the prosecution brought in his witnesses. They brought in the arresting officer and the building manager. I didn't think of anything I needed to ask the officer and the manager said she turned around didn't see anything so I made no cross examinations. My plan was to impeach the bellhop because he was the only witness against me and I had the indictment transcripts which showed he had claimed that the first time he had seen me was only a few weeks prior to the incident. That of course wasn't true and I had documents to prove that couldn't be true. I brought in my credit card statements that showed I had been in that area for almost SIX MONTHS and I brought in Mail addressed to me at that building, the Barclay 1755 York Ave, NY 10128. I had previously told the judge I intended to impeach the complaining witness which was a mistake because when I did he was ready for it and made a mockery of the impeachment. My constitutional right to a "neutral magistrate" was definitely not honored, the judge was prejudicial towards me and mislead the jury. It was a malicious prosecution and he knew it. He compared my legal rights of residency to a "squatter" in front of the jury despite the Tennant being in Love with me. He also liked to interrupt me which was a major distraction for the jury and made him appear bias against me. This requires reversal, See In re Murchison, 349 U.S. 133 (1955); Tumey v. Ohio, 273 U.S. 510 (1927). The trial was a sham. "The appearance of bias alone is grounds for reversal even if the trial judge is in fact, completely impartial.", Published Stanford law review, *The Appearance of Justice: Judges Verbal and Nonverbal Behavior in Criminal Jury Trials*, 38 Stan.L.Rev. 89 Nov. (1985). When it came time to make the cross examination of the complaining witness I asked him again when the first time he had seen me was and after he had already said a couple weeks in front of the jury, he changed his story. He then said he couldn't remember and the judge asked him if it was in 2011 or not and he said "I'm not sure". The complaining witness massively contradicted himself when he claimed it had been only two weeks and then admitted it could have been indefinitely longer than nine months. This was directly relevant to guilt or innocence because I was also being charged for trespassing and it was relevant to whether or not he could have possibly thought he had legal grounds to physically stop me. This violates the NY "Ledwon rule" which states a single testimony with inherent contradictions cannot establish proof beyond a reasonable doubt, See People v Ledwon, 153 NY 10 (1897). This rule is clearly supported by U.S. Supreme Court law in other words I think any judge should agree. After I enlightened the jury of the contradictions and said "the witness is impeached" the judge frantically stated it should be "stricken" from the record without explaining why. The jury then became confused and must have undermined the significance of the bellhop's inherent contradictions. He should have been charged for perjury. In many states they give jurors jury instructions on print for deliberation, they didn't do that and I don't think the jury understood the law or principle of self-defense. I Was ACQUITTED on Trespassing and found guilty on both counts of assault. Even a convicted felon has the Absolute right to run for President of The United States, See Franklin v. Murphy, 745 F.2d 1221 (9th Cir. 1984). I'm not sure why the jury didn't think if the law and facts required them to Acquit me on Trespassing it require them to Acquit me of assault. The judge stated three times on record that he Doubted sufficiency of evidence for the felony charge. Before trial I had walked over to the prosecutor's office and spoke to the prosecutor named kevin j. rooney from San Fransisco. He was a immoral tool and probably contributed to the complaining witness giving fabricated testimony to get the indictment. I informed him there was no justification for the prosecution and he refused to talk about it and just said he would use anything I said against me like piece of garbage who didn't care if I was innocent. He seemed like an immature juvenile who had no sense of right or wrong. During the trial he had a high pitched voice and sounded like he REALLY Wanted a career as a prosecutor. He also told the jury that they should convict me because I left Manhattan and moved back to Los Angeles. I was a lawful gun owner for over three years before this absurdity. I had to get rid of my guns because I would never risk going to jail for anything in the world. I purchased the transcripts out of pocket and retained Raiser & Kenniff to file a post trial motion to dismiss. I intentionally retained lawyers that liked to talk on TV. Tom Kenniff is on Youtube. The judge however denied the motion and I was sentenced to six months jail and five years probation. During my detainment and after release I out-litigated all the lawyers who had been on the case, See Taebel v. Sonberg 2:18 CV 00138-TLN (PS) Filed in Sacramento. As proof of conspiracy 18 U.S.C. §371 & §241the judge had intentionally misstated at the sentencing that probation was for a duration of "five months" and the private law firm sent me a letter that also said "five months". When I asked the lawyer about the letter he stated it was a "typo". I didn't find out that probation was for a duration of "five years" until after I was released.

I had never been to jail before, I knew I could handle myself but they don't usually fight fare. NYC has one of the largest and most dangerous jails in the world. However, the sentenced division is much safer because most of the inmates are there for misdemeanors. The unsentenced inmates may be getting ready to do serious time. I had to serve four of the six months and spent my time playing chess, cards and working out. We were able to have visits from friends and family and buy coffee and radios from commissary. We had outdoor recreation and weights in the yard. I was one of the strongest guys there and could out bench everyone my size. I was putting up the heaviest bar, 235 lbs 15 times. I lived in large rooms with up to seventy five people, no privacy. Most of the time I got along with everyone however once I had a problem with someone steeling my commissary. I got into a fight and spent a month in the box. The black detention officer wrote on the report that I called him a "nigger", which I did not. In that area of the jail you only go outside with other inmates one hour a day. There I began to write about my case and drafted another motion to dismiss. I still had access to the law library and a type writer so I wrote a 440.10 Motion to Dismiss. After I was released I personally delivered the five page motion to the clerk of court. Later I filed a supplemental affidavit that was another seventeen pages without transcripts. I had been confronted with such unjustified stupidity I declared in that motion my intent to be a politician. I hoped that would fix their misconceptions. It was a "Conspiracy" and "Kidnapping", See 18 U.S.C. §371 And 18 U.S.C. §1201. The indictment number is 2536/12. I started to think I was being prosecuted to control my future in politics which would would explain why I was unlawfully arrested the day after becoming of age to run for congress. My parents and little sister flew out to see me. The probation not only prevented me from leaving NY it confined me to the city limits. I tried to get the probation sentence stayed so I filed a New York Criminal Procedure Law § 450.60 motion with the appellate court however it was denied. While I was in the process of trying to get the probation transferred back to California the judge found an invalid reason to find a violation of the terms of probation. I had to share a house with a serial killer who killed two women and made my skin crawl so I punched him in the face. Then we wrestled and I got him in a headlock and he went for my testicles so I wrenched harder. A couple of detention officers broke it up. While I was in jail I opted to stay in protective custody where all the intelligent inmates stayed which allowed me to stay in Manhattan and off Riker's Island. The NYC corrections is one of the biggest and most dangerous jails in the World. I mostly stayed in Manhattan between Wall Street and the U.N. Headquarters and listening to political talk radio eight hours per day. Inmates each had their own cell. I listened to Sean Hannity, Michael Savage, Rush Limbaugh, Mark Levin, John Batchelor and more. I figured that it could beneficial to getting my charges overturned to have some political insight. I also had seen a few guys with big scars up and down their face in "general population" and I thought it would be a good idea. I read *"Unprecedented: The Constitutional Challenge to Obamacare"* by Josh Blackman. At one point they pulled me out of protective custody and I was forced to go to the Riker's Island. I fought like five people at one time. I laid a big black guy out and lifted his feet off the ground with one punch then he landed on his back. I got punched in the kidneys from behind then hit in the face and got six stitches under my left eye. I wrote to a lawyer named "Plastic Ben" who filed a Million dollar Lawsuit but when I told him I thought they were trying to kill me and asked him to make it $25 Million he got scared and dropped the lawsuit. I was then sentenced to one year in the Sing Sing prison after reading a book about it titled *"Newjack: Guarding Sing Sing"* by Ted Conover. It was about a journalist who worked one year as a correction officer then quit and wrote a book. I went ten days without food in protest against prison. I got down to 145 lbs. And I didn't shower for two weeks because I hated it there and didn't want to get raped. This was rational because arguably the more respectable a man the more he would detest being deprived of Liberty.

I used to think I was a democrat before I became educated on law and politics. I voted for Obama first term. Some of my favorite U.S. Supreme Court judges considered themselves progressive or liberal. The problem with the democrats is they are now socialists and I've thought socialism was a bad idea since Joseph Stalin and Adolf Hitler killed tens of millions of people. The Nazi party was named the "National Socialist German Workers' Party". Tucker Carlson reports that a number of major media sources have accepted money from totalitarian communist China and are therefore presenting propaganda. This is probably the tip of the ice berg. I don't think most of the democrats are evil and secretly know their policies are wrong. I think most of them are just ignorant and I have a responsibility to help educate them. I think there are however bad people that use the democratic ideals to extort the country. Some of them are just bad people and their intentions are against the welfare of the world. I think the democrats are emotionally driven. They are compelled by primitive feelings or hearsay rather than reason. Any proposal to raise taxes is preposterous. I think these arrests are from parasites who usually have liberal views. It's too much government and that's what the democrats associate with. If they don't kill you they will deprive you of liberty which is much worse than death. I would trust the opulent before I trust big government. Sometimes I think this is reverse discrimination by homosexuals for being straight. Sometimes I also think I've been prejudiced for my German heritage which I can do nothing about. Adolf Hitler was an idiot. My grandfather in law Samuel Chaitkin was a jew and we used to hang out and play cards. "Whenever you put your faith in big government for any reason, sooner or later you end up an apologist for mass murder" = Karl Hess. I believe in strongly the wisdom in our founding fathers who stressed the importance of a separation of powers and a very limited central government. My half brother Ryan Taebel the cop became a severe alcoholic while I was unlawfully detained. He died in 2015 from liver sclerosis. I never got a chance to help him or see him in the hospital because I was unlawfully in jail. I'm sure I would have saved his life.

When I was released in late 2015 I still had a year of parole which I transferred back to the Midwest to live with my parents at the lake house. Raquel Toro who was living with her mother and pursuing acting came to live with us for about six months. Royalty has lived with their parents for thousands of years. Cera Chastain from Colorado Mountain College came to visit me on a road trip across country. I got on "Tinder" and had a few hot dates. Hannah R. reached down my pants and wrapped her little fingers around my big cock on the Dance floor in front of everyone at Matey's a bar in Michigan City. Also at this Bar on another occasion I saw a man about sixty fucking a woman bent over in the back of an SUV while he stood under the open tailgate. He looked back at me and acted as if he was saying "You can hit it too" but I passed. I put "Best of Fall" on DVD on the market through Amazon's publishing program "Create Space". The Film was later taken down June of 2021 when create space discontinued their support for DVD media and I made Best of Fall public on Youtube. The creative documentary has no dialogue but has excellent cinematography. And it won an award. I spent time taking people fishing that year and fishing myself between trips. I am the CEO and Owner of "NORTHERN INDIANA GUIDE SERVICE". Taking people fishing is fun. It is a seasonal business. My rates are for one to two people are $200 a half day and $300 a full day and $100 for each additional angler. On good days I often get a $100 tip. I provide all the gear. The work is seasonal. I like fishing but I'm not into Hunting. We have Deer in my neighborhood and they are beautiful creatures. I took a girl named Amanda I met on Tinder fishing with me that summer and we used to have sex on the river all the time. I bought red 2014 Jeep Grand Cherokee Limited 4x4 in an auction on e bay. I began taking friends off-roading and was soon modifying my jeep. I would take girls on dates then off-roading and have sex with them in the back seat. I became a member of Jeepforum.com and wk2jeeps.com which were both very helpful. I posted under the alias of Limited9627. I personally installed a lift and new suspension on the jeep. I got custom Icon Vehicle Dynamic Coil-overs for the front and OME heavy springs and shocks for the back. I bought off-road steel rims and painted them camo tan to match the interior and put over size 265/70 R17 (31.6") Mastercraft Courser AXT All-Terrain tires on them. Whenever I paid anyone to work on the jeep I stayed there and watched them so I could learn everything I could. I took an online IQ test with my mother and the results said I was "Genius".

Her test results were not as high as mine. She says the day I was born was the best day of her life and it still was good for our relationship her knowing that. I figured it should be good for career opportunities to tell the world. My father made millions and I've been beating him in chess since I was seven years old. I wanted to go to the Trump-Pence rally in Fort Wayne but the parole officer wouldn't consent to it which I think was entirely unreasonable. All the while I had an appeal pending in the courts. When the state appeal was denied I filed a Federal habeas corpus, See Taebel v. Sonberg 18-1883 (2nd Cir.)

A number of entertainers have felonies and they may have actually been guilty. Tim Allen was arrested at the Kalamazoo Battle Creek International Airport in 1978 with 650 grams of cocaine. He plead guilty to a felony of drug trafficking. He served two years at the Federal Correctional Institution in Sandston, Minnesota. Mark Wahlberg punched an Asian guy and permanently blinded him in one eye. He was charged for attempted murder and plead guilty to felony assault with a two year sentence however only served forty five days of his sentence. He also dedicated his Memoir "Marky Mark" to his penis. In 2004 Martha Stewart was found guilty by jury trial of felony conspiracy, obstruction of an agency proceeding, and making false statements to federal investigators. She served five months in a federal correctional facility with two years of supervised release. Christian Slater was arrested in 1994 for attempting to board a commercial airplane with a gun in his luggage. He was also arrested in 1997 for punching someone and assaulting a police officer while under the influence of heroin, cocaine and alcohol. He is a Director, Producer and Actor. Robert Downey Jr. was arrested in 1996 for possession of cocaine, heroin and a 357 magnum in his vehicle. He plead guilty to a felony drug conviction and possession of a concealed weapon with a prior. He served one year and three months in prison and is now one of the Most Successful

Actors in Hollywood.

In October of 2016 I moved back to Los Angeles, This time Raquel Toro went with me. We found a superb sublet studio downtown at the SP Manhattan off 6th St. and Spring St. I set up a green screen in the studio and starting filming reels. It was in a great area with a lot of night clubs and on the roof there was a swimming pool and Jacuzzi. Our studio was on the third floor and I could see people lined up around the block to get into "Exchange LA" every Friday and Saturday night. I went to Clifton's, The Reserve, Honeycut, The Nest, Seven Grand, Golden Gopher, Broadway Bar, Fish, The Standard, The Ace and more. I also went to the W in Hollywood and the Bungalows in Santa Monica. On Halloween Clifton's let me in to a $250 cover party for free. I met Tori Spelling at Clifton's having lunch one day. The manager of Exchange LA also let me in for free one night. I bought twenty suits that year. I made a demo reel with scenes from Iron Man II, Wolf of Wall Street, Wall Street, Gladiator and I made up scenes for a Prosecutor and Game Show Host. I made a voice over demo with voices from Troy, The Dark Knight and a Sports Announcer. I designed Four websites. I started a production company. I am the CEO And Owner of "EPIC PRODUCTIONS" and "WESTERN STUDIOS". After the inauguration of Donald Trump there were marches in the streets by the democrats. I set up my camera on a tripod and began interviewing the protesters. After speaking with a handful of people I went back to the studio and started editing the footage, then I drove to CNN but they were closed. I looked like a top notch Journalist. I later named the film "LOGIC-Interviewing The Inauguration Protesters For The Basis of Their Opinions". I spent a few thousand dollars submitting a few of my films to the film festivals around the World. Logic received "Honorable Mention" from the "LOS ANGELES FILM AWARDS" February 2017. And "BEST OF FALL" Won First Place in Toronto, Canada. I walked into Paradigm Talent Agency to give them my resume with a DVD of my demo and commercial reel. I mailed copies to William Morris Endeavor and Creative Artists Agency. I also film demo reels for Actors for $500 each. I got back in shape and was 170lbs benching almost 300lbs and curling 85lb Dumbbells. That summer I went to pool bars across the city. I made a little money hosting acting classes off meetup.com. I sang Karaoke for the first time with a professional singer I met and it was awesome. I started playing Flag Football Sunday Mornings on the Beach in Santa Monica with a group I found on meetup.com. I also played Full time Quarterback with some College Players just North of the Santa Monica Pier. We went to a number of screenings that year through the SAG-AFTRA Union. I tried to get into Canda but was stopped at the border and denied access because of the unlawful conviction in NY. I went to Mexico every couple of months. I would go to Zona Norte in Tijuana where I fucked two girls on stage with a dildo while a hundred others girls stood around at the Hong Kong Nightclub. In Tijuana you can lawfully have sex with five girls for $100. My favorite Hotel Casinos were The Aria, The Cosmopolitan, The Bellagio, The Westin, The Mirage, The Venetian and The LINQ. I had sex with a girl against the ice machine at Harrah's. In September I scheduled Football games in major cities across the U.S. for an October road trip. I was thinking about finding someone to take over the sublet for a month or two but we ended up giving up the apartment which I regret. In October we traveled east and I Quarterbacked Flag Football Games along the way. In New Orleans I had sex with three girls at once in my Hotel room at the Le Méridien Hotel Downtown. When I was visiting the midwest I went to gyms in Chicago with two pairs of boxing gloves and mouth guards and found a few innocent guys who were willing to box. In late 2017 I applied to the Presidential Administration through the whitehouse.gov website as an advisor or general policy implementer. I sent them links to my website mitchtaebel.us and to my award winning documentary "Logic". On my way back to California between San Antonio and El Paso my vehicles computer went haywire and I had to have the vehicle towed. A diagnostic reported about one hundred error codes. Chrysler recommended a new engine. I got a second opinion and they said the same thing so I had a new engine installed. I think the onboard computer was hacked through satellite and the vehicle was sabotaged because of all the error codes and the fact that my wipers turned on in a peculiar way, moving up and down very slowly. A second time my computer was hacked and my vehicle entered four-low while I was in a dirt parking lot. I did a donut and put the vehicle back in four-high. I emailed fire fighters and police and invited them to play Flag-Football. I found a video online when I was researching global power that said the Illuminati wants to kill 6 billion people. The video was well done and had a little supporting evidence primarily the "Georgia Guidestones" which in eight languages call to limit the world population to under 500,000,000 and should definitely be taken Down. I found it concerning and showed a bunch of people. The video was censored on facebook and taken out of news feeds and now appears to have been taken down completely. When I saw Donald Trump on TV talking about prosecuting the states for cannabis I thought that was crazy and filed a Constitutional challenge against all federal laws criminalizing marijuana and sued Paul Ryan and Rex Tillerson, See 3:2018cv00014 in the Northern District of Indiana. Then Canada Legalized it. I started to look into colleges for the spring semester however my options were limited. I looked at the London Film Schools for the summer and was offered a scholarship into the Met Film School Masters program. I also applied to UCSD and UCSF for the fall because they would not accept application for the 2018 spring semester. I should have applied to UCLA. I ended up enrolling at one of the biggest universities in the country ASU (Arizona State University) as a Film and Media Production Major. The

University has been attended by too many Celebrities to list. There will be a link on my website. To name just a few David Spade (Actor, Comedian), Jimmy Kimmel (TV Host, Comedian), Michael R. Burns (Vice Chairman of Liongate), Theodore Anthony Sarandos Jr. (Chief Content Officer for Netfix), Doug Ducey (Governor, News Reporter), Dina Eastwood (News Anchor, Actress), Nick Nolte (Actor), Derrick Martin Hall (CEO Diamondbacks), Ryan Wood (Co-founder of Under Armour), Danny White(NFL Quarterback) and Cain Velasquez (two time UFC Heavyweight Champion). My intentions were to find a production crew and make a film for my portfolio. I only intended to take One semester of classes and then work with a production company as an assistant director or production assistant. I felt advanced after working on many Major Hollywood productions and already having Won two Film Awards. The class was a complete joke. I told them I was ready to film but their priority was only passing the class not Film Making. I wanted to make a Film about the Civil Rights Act and they wanted to make a film about a "taco stand". As Matthew McConaughey wrote in his Memoir "Greenlights" production companies don't care about a degree they might care about a great portfolio. I had this tremendous urge to quit the class and drive back to Los Angeles the first day of class but I didn't do it and I regret it. I met the Arizona Diamondbacks at a Nightclub in Tucson the weekend before I protested an illegal traffic stop.

CHAPTER 4

On January 24th of 2018 is when this illegal traffic stop and subsequent unjustified arrest occurred. I had just got a text from my mother who sent me her credit card info so I could buy a ticket that afternoon to fly into Chicago. I was on my way to the airport and I was kidnapped to prevent me from prosecuting all the lawsuits from a secure location. Before the unlawful attempted traffic stop someone hacked my Youtube account and took down the Film *LOGIC*. They took it down because they wanted to kidnap me and most judges would immediately release a Journalist or Award Winning Political Filmmaker. I was driving on cruise control and doing the speed limit of 55mph and not in a hurry. My plane didn't leave for four hours. I was "driving perfectly" as I stated to police after the arrest. I had reason to believe the officer was following me because of the lawsuits that I had filed. I filed a $1 billion lawsuit THAT MORNING, See Taebel v. Brown et al 1:18cv00192-TWP-MJD. Kamala Harris is a respondent in the lawsuit. I sued her for her negligence as the California Attorney General before she was a Senator. In the lawsuit I was demanding an arresting officer be charged and "executed by law" for kidnapping. I had filed a Constitutional Challenge arguing that the DOJ was unconstitutional and part of it should be SHUT DOWN, See Taebel v. U.S., 1:18-CV-00025-VJW filed in the U.S. Court of Federal Claims. The Wall Street journal wrote an article about the Lawsuit. I tend to think law enforcement just sit around spying on people and following them with or without a warrant and follow people, See Katz v. United States, 389 U.S. 347 (1967); Kyllo v. United States, 533 U.S. 27 (2001); United States v. Jones, 565 U.S. 400 (2012); Spinelli v. U.S., 393 U.S. 410 (1969). I was driving south bound on state road 85 to go to the Maricopa Train station but found out the train only runs every other day and the next train wasn't until the next day. I then turned around to head to the Phoenix airport and after a few minutes I saw the officer up ahead driving slowly. I thought the officer had been following me and wanted to pull me over from the moment I saw him because he was driving 10mph under the speed limit as if he was waiting for me to pass him. It seemed likely more than a coincidence that an officer wanted to make an illegal stop in a rural area the after filing a number of lawsuits and on my way out of town. I thought he was driving a detective's car because highway patrol vehicles are usually top of the line and work under a governor. He was driving a 2008 ten year old unmarked black Crown Victoria and I thought he was a mob police stalking me. He could have been following me on GPS. I had a very rational reason to think so after LOGIC was taken down, after my Jeep's computer was hacked, after all the lawsuits I filed and the Constitutional Challenge, after making reports of the malicious prosecution in NY to the U.S. government, after applying to the Presidential Administration and after writing all 50 governors about a State Convention. Any one of those could be a reason for unlawful surveillance. It is impossible to rationally argue that it wasn't a reasonable concern considering the circumstances and the evidence I have presented in this Book. Anyone should understand why a highly intelligent and reasonable person in that position might feel safer taking steps to lawfully protest the stop as I did by calling the Media, the Mayor, 911 and driving with traffic. I didn't know for sure wether it was a kidnapping nevertheless I decided to protest the unlawful traffic stop. The law says if a person is driving normally and refuse to stop officers are prohibited from using deadly force, See Brower v. County of Inyo, 489 U.S. 593 (1989); Tennessee v. Garner, 471 U.S. 1 (1985). An unlawful arrest whether or not intentional is kidnapping. If it was intentional or reckless then someone should be prosecuted and that's definitely kidnapping. The risk of stopping was that I would have had an officer who was already incriminating himself standing next to me with a gun and that I could have been shot without any witnesses, See U.S. v. Price, 383 U.S. 787 (1966) or he could have planted drugs on me which would be hard to make a defense against, See Manning v. Miller, 355 F.3d 1028 (7th Cir. 2004); Limone v. Condon, 372 F.3d 39 (1st Cir. 2004). Police are also known to start physical confrontation and then claim to have been assaulted. The fact of the matter is that I had a reasons to believe my life could be in danger and an illegal traffic stop is a criminal offense under The Civil Rights Act, "those lawfully within the country, entitled to use the public highways, have a right to free passage without interruption or search unless there is known to a competent official, authorized to search, probable cause for believing that their vehicles are carrying contraband or illegal merchandise.", See Almeida-Sanchez v. United States, 413 U.S. 266 (1973). Supreme Court of The United States rulings are the law of the Land. Here, the court affirmed that it is a criminal offense for the government to violate a Supreme Court ruling, See Screws v. United States, 325 U.S. 91 (1945). One criminal offense is often followed by another. I really didn't feel safe stopping under the circumstances. I asked the 911 dispatcher and the negotiator who called me for the reason for the stop and they were either unwilling or unable to provide one. An officer only needs reasonable suspicion to make a traffic stop however it can't be based on feelings or a hunch an officer needs "specific articulable facts" indicating a crime has been committed, See United States v. Brignoni-Ponce, 422 U.S. 873 (1975); Brown v. Texas, 443 U.S. 47 (1979); Florida v. J.L., 529 U.S. 266 (2000). This is how I knew they couldn't possibly have a valid reason to make a stop. I thought it was at the very least an invalid reasonable suspicion stop or at worst a threat to my life. The officer made false statements alleging two traffic violations which was false and an implausible. It only takes one traffic violation for an officer to pull someone over so the allegation that the officer witnessed not one but two traffic violations on a rural road before he attempted to pull me over is implausible on it's face. It only takes a second to activate an officer's lights. The officer claimed I was speeding and made an unsafe lane change. I was driving carefully doing the speed limit exactly and definitely not committing a new traffic violation every ten seconds as that officer's statements would lead you to believe, See Manuel v. City of Joliet, Ill., 580 S. Ct. 911 (2017). My refusal to stop didn't cause the endangerment of the public or an accident, excessive illegal force by law enforcement did. No one used spike strips against O.J. Simpson in the summer of 1994, officers did not assault him in his vehicle, they even had a warrant for murder. No one is supposed to get crazy over an alleged traffic violation. That case got 150 Million Viewers. The Trump v Biden Presidential debate got 73 Million viewers. A refusal to comply with a "lawful" traffic stop is only a class 2 misdemeanor, See A.R.S. § 28-622; Orn v. City of Tacoma, 949 F.3d 1167 (9th Cir. 2020). "Deadly force" cannot be used to apprehend a misdemeanant offender even if they had a lawful reason to make a stop, See Tennessee v. Garner, 471 U.S. 1 (1985). Officers deployed approximately seven spike strips on I-10 which I circumvented. The speed limit on that highway is 75mph, spike strips are dangerous and at that speed they are "deadly force". This was constitutionally unreasonable. Ten people died because of one spike strip in a vehicle traveling only "about 45 miles per hour", See U.S. v. Pineda-Doval, 614 F.3d 1019 (9th Cir. 2010). I was well within my legal rights to resist the unlawful arrest after the use of excessive force even if the officer had had a lawful reason to make a stop in the first place, See A.R.S. 13-404B(2); Badelk v. United States, 177 U.S. 529 (1900). If the use of a K-9 is considered deadly force then the use of spike strips on the highway is absolutely "deadly force", See Smith v. City of Hemet, 394 F.3d 689 (9th Cir. 2005). Deadly force wasn't justified or lawful, See Tennessee v. Garner, 471 U.S. 1 (1985). Even a high speed pursuit that could endanger the public doesn't warrant deadly force as ruled by a unanimous Supreme Court of the United States, See Brower v. County of Inyo, 489 U.S. 593 (1989). The use of spike strips was excessive force and "attempted murder" by law enforcement, See 18 U.S.C. 1113; 18 U.S.C. §241 & §242. The three helicopter videos show I was driving with traffic for almost an hour and stopping at red lights before an officer assaulted my vehicle. He attempted to roll my vehicle with an illegal PIT which was assault with a "dangerous weapon", See 18 U.S.C. §241 & §242. The use of a PIT was ruled to be unconstitutional in most circumstances including this one, See Scott v. Harris, 550 U.S. 372 (2007)(W/Dissent). It was Felony assault by officers on Television. Force used by an officer must be "necessary" by Arizona law, See A.R.S. 13-209. As the police reports and video show at the time of unlawful arrest at least four tasers were used simultaneously which was deadly and excessive force against someone who wasn't resisting, See Glasscox v. City of Argo, No. 16-16804 (11th Cir. 2018); Oliver v. Florino, 586 F.3d 898 (11th Cir. 2009). The police reports also stated multiple times that I struck the police cruiser with my vehicle. The video clearly shows an officer striking the back of my vehicle with the front of his. This is proof we have a tyrannical government where police think they can put blatantly false statements in police reports without fear of being sued or prosecuted and fired. This was perjury and intentional "kidnapping" by officers, See 18 U.S.C. §1201; 18 U.S.C. 241 &242. These problems don't get better when people don't talk about them. It is solicitation to future excessive force and homicides by officers not to prosecute them for their violations of the law. The most dangerous fact is the mentality it promotes within law enforcement for the Media and Public not to take action against such unjustified conduct. Equal protections of law requires that they be charged. The Constitution require that they be charged, See Koon v. U.S., 518 U.S. 81 (1996). It was a failure of the Duty of douglas ducey the governor, mark brnovich the attorney general, william gerard montgomery the county attorney and the U.S. Government. The police were probably embarrassed and pressing hard to keep me detained because they appeared as if they couldn't do anything right on television. One, I gracefully avoided seven spike strips. Two, they failed at boxing me in. Three, they made and unsuccessful and illegal PIT maneuver. Four, they caused an accident with an innocent driver. Five, after the accident I got out of my vehicle and stood on the sidewalk while a police officer looked in my vehicle and all around for me. He didn't know I was the driver he thought I was a bystander. Six, they realized I had a justifiable reason not to think I was being kidnapped. Some knew and others didn't. The problem with stupid people is they don't DETEST unjustified or unlawful arrests as they should. Smart people like Supreme Court Judges or Congress who made it a Capitol offense do!

In the Fifteen Minute Press Statement that Aired on National Television I said a number of things in my Defense. I said there was "no probable cause... no reasonable suspicion... or a traffic violation... I called the Mayor... I also called 911... I told them they were attempting to make an unlawful arrest... call officers back. Their officers did turn off their lights and back off for a bit... an unmarked vehicle attacked me abruptly... so I sped off to you know resist the unlawful arrest and an accident ensued... A detective called me after I called 911. He was not able to tell me why they were attempting to make a stop in the first place. He could not justify probable cause there was none what so ever... He couldn't have a reasonable conversation about why they wanted to stop me... I would like to either get... a pro bono Federal Civil Lawyer or I have a relative Scott Taebel in Wisconsin who could file a suit from Chicago and subpoena all the evidence from the case including the 911 call, including the conversation with the detective, the phone call to the Mayor was probably recorded, they can subpoena all the helicopter camera footage and the police reports and anything that's been written down by the District Attorney's Office. So I'd like to file a suit against the City and against the District Attorney's Office... and file for a Federal Injunction against any prosecution coming from the City if they do not immediately drop the charges... JOURNALIST: Did you have anything inside your car? Any stolen items? MY RESPONSE: Negative. I'm not a criminal at all. If you have the impression that I've been arrested look at the federal case laws that I have... I've... had several issues with police before for being charged for things that I was absolutely innocent of and I'm filing suits against them for those arrests so there seems to be a pattern here of several arrests against me for things I have not done they're all in the federal courts it's all out there for everybody to review and this is another perfect example of being stopped and arrested for something that I did not do and without reasonable cause so the police are out of line here, they need better training furthermore there is... federal law 18 USC Section 241 and 242 that protects citizens rights of America to a high degree and they say arrests without probable cause can be considered kidnapping or attempted kidnapping for prosecutions as well, it can warrant life in prison it can warrant the death penalty so that is one of the greatest laws ever written to uphold the US Constitution and they can be charged including the prosecutors under this section if they do not drop the charges and release me immediately. JOURNALIST: when you've got off the freeway... were you worried about hurting anyone else? MY RESPONSE: Absolutely... one of the things I said to the police to the 911 operator it was on the message they should pull that and make it public here's my verbal consent was I didn't want to jeopardize anyone's safety on the road and I said that to the detective I said call the officers back I don't want to attack me I don't want to jeopardize anyone's safety they were throwing spike strips... at me along the road as I was just driving along I wasn't really running I was just kind of driving along and moving out of the way... I have a website MITCHTAEBEL.US it has links to my production websites to my photography websites to a number of things I've done... JOURNALIST: why do you ask the officer why he was stopping you to avoid this whole mess? MY RESPONSE: I was concerned that it was going to result in some kind of unlawful arrest... I wasn't going to stop for the guy and there was no reason to stop me because there was no traffic violation... I turned back around to go to the Phoenix Airport to fly back to Chicago that's what I was doing. I don't know what this officer was out there doing or why he attempted to stop me but he had no valid reason what so ever... I made a 911 report that I thought corrupt police officers were attempting to make an unlawful arrest... unmarked vehicles made an abrupt turn to block me in and the other one just BASHED into the back of me so I was abruptly attacked and I just you know sped off to resist the unlawful arrest so it's unfortunate that anyone else had to be involved in an accident I said it twice I said to the 911 call and I said to the detective you called me and I may have said it a third time to the mayor I really didn't want anything to happen they had no reason to make an aggressive stop or throw spike strips completely unreasonable there wasn't like a big crime... that doesn't really make sense why they would want to actively aggressively chase somebody down who doesn't want to stop and believes their under unlawful attempted unlawful arrest and who's calling 911 explaining that to them so they know who I am they have my phone they have my license plate they have my identity if they want to pull a warrant for like a speeding ticket go ahead but you don't aggressively chase people and pursue them because it just instigates issues and can cause problems and jeopardize the safety of other people and I said it several times I didn't want that to happen... so I think the police and the City should be held liable for her accident for my accident I will be filing suit against them and she should as well... I don't know where the Mayor is I called the Mayor's office... If you review the video footage on the highway I was hardly speeding just driving along... I had to speed off... when you call 911 they can get in touch with state police they can get in touch with City police... I'm All American I've got to get bailed out... I'd like to do this in finer clothes and not in an orange jump suit and handcuffs... police can't go around harassing people to be the man okay thats what they attempt to do... Where is the dash cam of the illegal lane change... JOURNALIST: how many cases like this have you won? MY RESPONSE: okay that's it we're wrapped up today so ladies and gentlemen thank you very much for coming". Some of my favorite quotes from commentators were: "Future Senator standing there!!"- Offgrid J., "Take a shot every time this guy says unlawful."-The Taino Warrior, "People he is right, you are ten times more likely to be killed by police than a terrorist"- Mark V., "100% OF WHAT HE SAYS IS TRUE!! LIKE IT OR NOT!!"- ROOFER T., "This guys great. Spot on. That most have no clue as to what he is saying/doing is proof of the brainwashing we've all gone thru..."-Victor E., "Trump's legal team Leader"-Jeffrey M., "highway patrol should have terminated the chase multiple times..."-Michael G., "He is absolutely right unlawful arrest MUST be resisted. Americans in the caliber of the founding fathers are coming out of the woodwork to resist this blatant tyranny and its scaring the hell out of the police/prison complex. God bless you Mitchell Taebel. You are a true patriot."- Anton W. and "This man is my hero. Finally standing up to the bullcrap police state we ALL LIVE IN! If we ALL took this kind of stand, WE COULD LIVE WITHOUT OPPRESSION."-Dana M.. Crystal Cruz from CBS Los Angeles who went to my sublet Down Town LA Apartment Building asking about me said I had earned my fame for "the wrong reasons" however this is more a reflection of who I was long before Arizona and what can happen when law enforcement kidnap a person who talks on TV for a living or a person who chose to take public speaking in College. The media's coverage of this story was only the tip of the iceberg and they didn't seem to get that I had been kidnapped for filing a lawsuit or understand there was a right to resist unlawful arrest. This could have been considered one of the biggest stories in U.S. History. I already had been on National TV a number of times, traveled around the World on Semester at Sea with Ivy League students that work in the White House, set a World Record at thirteen and was an Award Winning Political Filmmaker.

The ABC 15 News Article titled "HEAR THE CALL: Pursuit suspect calls 911 during chase that ended in terrifying crash" by Dave Biscobing posted February 6th, 2018 and last updated February 07th, 2018 states: "Other than the 911 call, Goodyear had limited involvement in the pursuit. Dispatch logs reveal that goodyear chose not to assist in the DPS pursuit... DPS is facing questions about how it handled the pursuit and recent changes to the agency's pursuit policies... An internal investigation is going on". The Article then contains the 911 Transcripts which state: " TAEBEL: I am on the I-10. That's correct. DISPATCH: And the officers are following you? What kind of vehicle are you in? TAEBEL: I'm in a Grand Cherokee 2014... They actually have turned off their lights. They are not following me... let me first finish. First off, they are trying to stop me without probable cause. I was doing the speed limit, driving and they attempted to stop me without probable cause... I've called the Mayor's Office. They have my name. I told them the situation... I just want to make an official report of who I am... The last name is Taebel. First name is Mitch. I have several federal lawsuits against police that have stopped and made arrests, made stops without probable cause. You can search it online in the federal courts... I'm not stopping. There is no probable cause... I just want to let you know and ask your officers to back off... I don't want to jeopardize anyone's safety... (I ask her for the reason for the initial stop) DISPATCH: You were going over 80 mph on the I-10". I wasn't even on I-10 when the officer attempted to make the initial stop so that answer was invalid.

The Police Reports that have been filed in court a number of times and made public state in the "Synopsis": "On Wednesday, January 24, 2018, at approximately 0959 hours, Sargent Gilbert Federico, #4433, with the Arizona Department of Public Safety (DPS), attempted to conduct a traffic stop on a red 2014 Jeep Grand Cherokee (GC) for unsafe lane usage and speed on State Route 85 (SR-85), milepost 138. Sgt. Federico was driving an unmarked 2008 Ford Crown Victoria... The GC continued to disregard the emergency lights and continued onto Interstate 10 eastbound (I-10). There were several attempts with stop-sticks to deflate the GC's tires by DPS and Maricopa County Sheriff's Office but the GC evaded them. At approximately 1026 hours, Goodyear Police Department notified DPS a person who reported themselves as the driver of the GC had called 911 and they were talking to them. Goodyear PD 911 said they were trying to get the driver to pull over and he eventually hung up on them. At 1041 hours, a DPS negotiator contacted the driver of the GC... Taebel stated he did not want to stop due to the unlawfulness of the traffic stop and wanted a peaceful resolution to the incident... During this time, there was a police helicopter assisting with tracking the GC. Pursuing ground units shut down their emergency lights and allowed Taebel to drive ahead while the air unit monitored... Unmarked DPS police vehicles positioned themselves and attempted to box Taebel's vehicle while activating their emergency lights when he was stopped at Rio Solado Parkway and Scottsdale Road. Taebel struck one of the unmarked police vehicles with emergency lights which had two state Troopers and pushed it aside with his vehicle.". The "General Report" states: "At 1007 hours, Sergeant Federico reported the jeep missed the tire deflation devices (stop-sticks)... AZ DPS Trooper N. Mitchell, #6439, was set up for a stop-stick deployment on eastbound Interstate 10 (I-10)... the Jeep avoided the stop-sticks... AZ DPS Trooper R. Hicks, #6713, deployed his stop-sticks... but the attempt was unsuccessful... At 1019 hours, there was another unsuccessful attempt to use the stop-stick in a single stick deployment by AZ DPS Sergeant D. Felan, #6603... helicopter was above the patrol units... At 1030 hours the emergency vehicles backed off and shut down their emergency lights... At 1032 hours DPS Trooper D. Zamora, #6068, deployed his stop-sticks... and was unsuccessful... I reviewed video footage from 'Channel 3' news and saw the following take place at approximately 1051 hours... Troopers in unmarked vehicles, activated their emergency lights and attempted to box in Taebel's vehicle. Taebel accelerated and collided with an unmarked DPS vehicle... Taebel said he informed them that they would risk the public's safety if they pursued a high-speed chase or came after him and they did it anyway... He said he was not going to stop when he felt he did nothing wrong in a remote area and he was driving perfect... Taebel stated he told 911 that he did not want to jeopardize anyone's safety and to call the officers back and to handle this civilly... Taebel said there seemed to be an issue here with the police and suggested we should let him go right now. Taebel stated a violation of 18 USC section 242 could be considered kidnapping and can warrant capital punishment. Taebel informed me that since this was officially recorded the city should release him immediately. Taebel paused and then stated there is case law from the Supreme Court that people can resist unlawful arrest... Taebel went on to say, 'I know my Rights'... Taebel said the officer was aggressive and at that point he sped up to 'lawfully resist an unlawful arrest'". All the spike strips were not accounted for in the police reports as not all my property was accounted for. I think there were about seven spike strips. Additionally an officer in a Tahoe pulled up next to me and attempted throw a spike strip under my front right tire which I avoided. A dangerous maneuver that was already ruled illegal by the U.S. District Court in Arizona.

The Arizona Department of Public Safety "Pursuit Operations" Dated: February 15, 2006 states: "I(A): The Department's primary concern in pursuit driving is to protect the lives and safety of all citizens and troopers... III: Pursuit Commander Responsibilities... G: Terminate a pursuit when the necessity of apprehension is outweighed by the risks involved or the apprehension can be accomplished by other means... IX: Pursuit Procedures... G: When an aircraft is in position to monitor the pursuit, the pursuit commander shall determine the need for continuing emergency response operation by pursuing units and advise involved troopers... XII Authorized Intervention... D: The use of deadly physical force is justified only when the trooper reasonably believes it is necessary: 1: To defend himself/herself or a third person from what the trooper reasonably believes to be the use or imminent use of deadly physical force. 2: To effect an arrest or to prevent the escape from, custody of a person whom the trooper reasonably believes: a: Has committed, attempted, is committing, or attempting to commit a felony involving the use or threatened use of a deadly weapon. b: Is attempting to escape by use of a deadly weapon. c: Through past or present conduct of the person known to the trooper that the person is likely to endanger human life or cause serious physical injury unless apprehended without delay. d: Is necessary to lawfully suppress a riot if the person or another person participating in the riot is armed with a deadly weapon. (E): A Class C roadblock, ramming, and the shooting of a vehicle would be authorized only in situations where deadly physical force is justified. For the purposes of this order, ramming is defined as intentional contact by a police unit with a fleeing vehicle for the purpose of ending a pursuit. XIII: Pursuit Termination: A: Pursuits shall be terminated immediately when: 1: A pursuit commander, any sworn supervisor, or any commander orders the pursuit terminated. 2: A clear and unreasonable hazard exists to the trooper, fleeing suspect, or other citizens. 3: The pursuit leaves a controlled access highway into a densely populated or congested environment and the only known offense is a traffic infraction, misdemeanor, or non-violent felony, including felony flight. 4: The level of the criminal act does not justify the risk to life and property by the immediate apprehension of the suspect. B: Consideration should be given to terminating the pursuit when one or more of the following factors are present: 1: The pursuit leaves a controlled access highway into an area which is not densely populated and/or contains little or no vehicular traffic and the only known offense is a traffic infraction, misdemeanor, or non-violent felony, including felony flight. 2: The suspect identified to the point where later apprehension can be accomplished and continuing the pursuit would serve only to increase the risk to all involved. 3: Closing the distance between the trooper and suspect would require speeds that would place the trooper and public in danger. 4: The primary unit driver loses visual contact with the suspect. 5: Pursuits initiated by another agency and involving department units leave department jurisdiction. 6: Weather conditions that substantially increase the risk involved in continuing the pursuit. 7: The pursuing trooper is unfamiliar with the area and is unable to determine the location and/or direction of the pursuit accurately." That's Not just Arizona Policy that's U.S. Supreme Court of The United States Law. The Arizona Department of Public safety "Pursuit Operations" was changed to more vague restrictions on November 9th, 2017 just months before this unlawful arrest an kidnapping. The new manual still states: I: "Sworn personnel shall terminate pursuits when the risk outweighs the justification for immediate apprehension of the suspect". The changes in policy to avoid liability for officer's violent conduct has been criticized by the Media and Public and for good reason.

There is only one name anyone has to mention to completely discredit police, Abner Louima. In 1997 he was beaten by New York City Police Department Officers who shoved a broken broom stick up his rectum. This is clearly the facet of a much bigger problem. The officers responsible where charged and convicted in federal court. The officer who sexually assaulted him with a broom stick is still serving his thirty year sentence. In 2002 two police officers Dwaun Jabbar Guidry and Rolando Rico Trevino sexually assaulted five women and after an unlawful traffic stop raped another, See United States v. Guidry, 456 F.3d 493 (5th Cir. 2006). It is concerning to see how little the media covered this incident. I entered both the officer's names in YouTube and could not find any press coverage. Furthermore federal agents were found by a jury to have framed Steven Manning for the crimes of kidnapping and murder which he did not commit, See Manning v. Miller, 355 F.3d 1028 (7th Cir. 2004). Here, a Boston police officer was found by jury trial to have assisted the FBI in framing three men for a murder they did not commit, See Limone v. Condon, 372 F.3d 39 (1st Cir. 2004). The courts later awarded over $100,000,000 for the FBI's participation in the conspiracy, See Limone v. U.S., 579 F.3d 79 (1st Cir. 2009). There are hundreds if not thousands of cases like this where officers were found to have planted evidence that can be found online. A certain percentage of the population is more sociopathic than the rest. Those people are drawn to work in law enforcement. Sometimes people aren't suited to have authority, See *The Last King of Scotland* (2006). The federal government could have been in on it which would explain their failure to enforce the Civil Rights Act. Possibly because of the constitutional challenge I had filed alleging the "modern Doj" was excessive and unconstitutional before the kidnapping, See Taebel v. United States, No. 2018-1475 (United States Court of Appeals for the Federal Circuit); No. 1:18-CV-00025-VJW (U.S. Court of Federal Claims). I also demanded damages for deliberate indifference and failure to enforce the Civil Rights Act, See Taebel v. Doj, Case No. CV 18-06697-PA (JDE). I filed the constitutional challenge pursuant Federal Rules of Civil Procedure Rule 5.1 because I had reported the malicious prosecution in NYC and they failed to investigate or even respond and I suspected unlawful surveillance. Alex Jones believes the FBI is the biggest criminal organization in America. Once I listened to him talk about Facebook filtering news feeds and then I made a few posts from a second account and I confirmed the posts were in fact being filtered and not showing up viewable in the news feed of other accounts. It was proof that at least some of what he says is real. Ron Paul and Donald Trump also have both been on his show. WWII was an example of what happens when law enforcement has too much power. This book is about saving the world from another gestapo who caused the holocaust.

In many states as in Arizona the law requires officers to withdraw from a pursuit all together especially for a refusal to stop for a mere traffic violation, "During a pursuit, the need to apprehend the suspect should outweigh the level of danger created by the pursuit. When the immediate danger to the public created by the pursuit is greater than the immediate or potential danger to the public should the suspect remain at large, then the pursuit should be discontinued or terminated... Pursuits should usually be discontinued when the violator's identity has been established to the point that later apprehension can be accomplished without danger to the public", See Scott v. Harris, 550 U.S. 372 (2007) (Stevens): quoting Brief for Georgia Association of Chiefs of Police, Inc. The Supreme Court of The United States said one, two, three times "that courts must be closed to the trial of a crime instigated by the government's own agents.", See U.S v. Russell, 411 U.S. 423 (1973) (W/Dissents). "One has an undoubted right to resist an unlawful arrest", See U.S. v. Di Re, 332 U.S. 581 (1948). The laws of Nature and logic require that men have an absolute right to resist an unlawful arrest. If an officer can't make lawful arrests and abide by the minimum requirements of the law then he shouldn't be an officer. Arizona law explicitly states one has a right to use force in self-defense " whether the arrest is lawful or unlawful" when "physical force used by the peace officer exceeds that allowed by law", See A.R.S. 13-404B(2). Despite having very valid legal arguments, the state of Arizona appointed counsel against my will who acquiescence to a malicious prosecution with mental health allegations and failed to make any genuine defense. The state spent over three years claiming to be trying to figure out if I was competent to stand trial. All the while I was unconstitutionally detained. I never signed anything to allow these lawyers to represent me. The state cannot appoint counsel without the consent of a defendant, See Faretta v. California, 422 U.S. 806 (1975). "The right of personal liberty is one of the fundamental rights guaranteed to every citizen, and any unlawful interference with it may be resisted. Every person has a right to resist an unlawful arrest; and, in preventing such illegal restraint of his liberty, he may use such force as may be necessary.", See Wainwright v. City of New Orleans, 392 U.S. 598 (1968) (Warren): quoting Monroe v. Ducas, 203 La. 971, 14 So.2d 781 (1943). "Where the officer is killed in the course of the disorder which naturally accompanies an attempted arrest that is resisted, the law looks with very different eyes upon the transaction, when the officer had the right to make the arrest, from what it does if the officer had no such right. What might be murder in the first case might be nothing more than manslaughter in the other, or the facts might show that no offense had been committed.", See Badelk v. United States, 177 U.S. 529 (1900); See Also Jefferson D. Hughes III, *The Right to Resist Unlawful Arrest*, 38 La. L. Rev. (1978). To suggest that there wasn't a right to resist an illegal arrest is to promote the slavery of the modern human. It would also promote unlawful arrests. The Constitution requires the Courts to appose unlawful arrests one hundred percent. The right to force ably resist an unlawful arrest has been around since the Magna Carta in 1215 and still exists today across Europe, See Jonathan Herring, *Criminal*

Law 10th Edition, London, Palgrave Law Masters, Published 2017. "Citizens may resist unlawful arrest to the point of taking an arresting officer's life if necessary.", See Plummer v. State, 135 Ind 308 34 N.E. 968 (1893)(There seems to be false information on the internet regarding this quote and claims the quote does not exist in the case law however it most certainly does I took the quote directly from the ruling).The Media did a terrible job covering this story because they never talked about the clear assault by police captured on camera. I said the police should be held liable for the accident and they should have, See Natesway v. City of Tempe, 184 Ariz. 374 (1995); City of Scottsdale v. Kokaska, 17 Ariz.App. 120 (19720). I tried to get my insurance company to sue the police for the cost of both vehicles. After I made the press statement I realized I didn't say "assault" or "excessive force" directly but I had implied it when I said that the police should be held liable for the accident. Sometimes when I speak I make my points indirectly when I think it's obvious. Also when I write I sometimes like people to be able to connect the dots and draw the inferences. Necessity and facts. However, I expected a follow up press conference where I would be able to clarify my statements. I wanted to release all the evidence and have an ongoing debate about what happened. The Media was already at the police station waiting for me when I arrived and trying to ask me questions. After the press conference the next day, the press returned two days later. The guards brought another release waiver and asked me if I wanted to talk to the press again. I of course said yes I signed the waiver. Then, at last minute someone stopped the second press conference. I few days later there was a court order against press visitation for the remainder of the detainment.

As much as I appreciated the Media trying to help, they could have did a much better job. They were supposed to listen to every word I said like I was President and then do research and go ask the most knowledgable person in the country about it. CNN covered the story and brought on a bimbo defense Attorney named Anahita Sedaghatfar who did the worst job imaginable and gave a mind blowing stupid opinion. Passing the Bar exam is supposed to be the beginning of an attorney's legal studies however for most attorneys their legal research nearly ends when they graduate law school. CNN's Ashleigh Banfield said I "got to 150 miles an hour at times" however the Grand Cherokee tops out at 110 mph. If it wasn't a kidnapping I should have been released on bail. The Media said ASU employee who allegedly pointed me out to police later called the press and pointed out that I was driving non-dangerously until they assaulted me in a heavily populated area. None of my photos from Semester at Sea, Florida or High School were public on Facebook when this happened as they are now. That is why people are supposed to be released after an arrest so the accused can gather evidence and make it public. ABC was the only Network that even acknowledged that the police acted unethically but they could have did a lot more. No one identified the conduct as Felony assault by police on Television. They should have filed a suit against the unconstitutional Media preclusion order like they have in the past in cases where the defendants probably weren't kidnapped, See Pell v. Procunier, 417 U.S. 843 (1974); Saxbe v. Washington Post Co., 417 U.S. 843 (1974); Nebraska Press Association v. Stuart, 427 US 539 (1976). They should have been discussing the use of deadly force by police because excessive force automatically gives a person the right to resist the arrest. The media clearly needs more people with legal knowledge on their team. They should have interviewed Civil Rights Attorneys or Professors on the video footage. I guarantee they would have had to agree with everything I was saying. Law enforcement or the Media were also not supposed to list my prior arrests on television in order to make the unlawful arrest not look like a kidnapping. "Lawyers and law enforcement personnel should not volunteer the prior criminal records of an accused except to aid in his apprehension or to warn the public of any dangers he presents. The news media can obtain prior criminal records from the public records of the courts, police agencies and other governmental agencies and from their own files. The news media acknowledge, however, that publication or broadcast of an individual's criminal record can be prejudicial, and its publication or broadcast should be considered very carefully, particular after the filing of formal charges and as the time of the trial approaches, and such publication or broadcast should generally be avoided because readers, viewers and listeners are potential jurors and an accused is presumed innocent until proven guilty.", See Nebraska Press Association v. Stuart, 427 US 539 (1976) (Brennan, Stewart and Marshall, Concurring). Furthermore, many of the arrests mentioned on TV were dismissed or declined by the prosecutor. Legal kidnappings presented as valid arrests for no other reason than to discredit me, See Hutchinson v. Proxmire, 443 U.S. 111 (1979). Furthermore, I do not consider my self a "sovereign citizen" as law enforcement claimed I had said I was. That term is not in the legal dictionary and there doesn't appear to be any accepted validity to the beliefs associated with the term. I had never heard of it until it was being alleged I claimed to be one. I assumed it was made up in an attempt to discredit me and my valid legal views. I did say that the arresting officers could be "killed" for "Kidnapping" me under the Civil Rights Act because that's what it says, See 18 U.S.C. §241 & §242. Captitol punishment is the strongest form of crime deterrent which is the only reason I said that. It seems natural to me that a man that knew that would say it if he was being unjustly arrested or kidnapped. The better a man the more he must detest this kind of conduct by law enforcement like the most respectable Supreme Court of The United States judges. I am a person that is sophisticated and makes sense. Everything I do has a reason. I'm not by any means an extremist. I base my legal views on the most official sources possible, primarily the words of the Constitution and U.S. Supreme Court rulings and then Congressional Legislative law.

CHAPTER 5

The good, the powerful and the highly intelligent have all been unjustly arrested. Liu Xiaobo won The Nobel Peace Prize in 2010 and recently died from liver cancer while in Chinese government custody July 13th 2017. He had been to prison a number of times. Martin Luther King, Jr. won The Nobel Peace Prize in 1964 and was arrested numerous times. Aung San Suu Kyi won The Nobel Peace Prize in 1991 and later became the equivalent of Prime Minister of Burma. She spent almost fifteen years on house arrest. Nelson Mandela received The Nobel Peace Prize in 1993 and served as President of South Africa from 1994-1999. He was a prisoner for twenty seven years. Vaclav Havel, a playwright and human rights campaigner was imprisoned between 1979-1983 and won the Presidential Election of Czechoslovakia in 1989 then the Presidential Election of The Czech Republic in 1993. John Lewis was arrested forty times before he was elected to The United States House of Representatives in Georgia. There are many more. Jesus was unconstitutionally arrested before he was killed, See Acts 1:16 and Mark 15:25.

The conditions of the Maricopa county jail were atrocious. Every day we wondered if there was going to be genocide. I definitely wasn't the only one who thought that. I remember this girl at court screaming "they are going to kill me! I just know it!". There was no outdoor access or direct sunlight. The ninth Circuit has ruled that a prisoner's forty five minutes of outdoor exercise per week for a six-week period was unconstitutional, See Lopez v. Smith, 203 F.3d 1122 (9th Cir. 2000). They gave the inmates pink underwear and pink handcuffs like the place was run by homosexuals who wanted everyone to look gay. A few weeks after the kidnapping a Tempe police officer brought me a no trespassing warning stating that I could not return to ASU until the case was resolved. I heard somewhere that someone had claimed I had been expelled but I never heard that until after the kidnapping. If anyone said that it was part of the conspiracy. There were no visitation by friends or family. I wished I was dead every day for over three years. Which is why the law requires everyone be released on reasonable bail with very few exceptions and I definitely wasn't one of them. The detainment in Arizona was much worse than NY because I didn't know when I was going to get out. The conditions of the jail were in violation of the Supreme Court Ruling which ruled "Punitive" pre-trial detainment was unconstitutional, See Bell v Wolfish, 441 U.S. 520 (1979)(W/Dissents). There were no type writers or pens like there were in NY in Arizona they provided golf size pencils without means to sharpen them. When I learned to soak the pencils in water until they cracked then remove the lead and sharpen them with nail files then put the pencil back together with rubber bans or hair ties I started filing paper with very valid legal arguments in the courts. I filed tens of thousands of pages in State and Federal Courts with exhibits. I filed a billion dollar suit against the governor and the jail captains and shift commanders for the conditions and the complaints served by deputies upon the defendants, See Taebel v. Ducey et al 19-16169 (U.S. 9th Cir.). A few months later they brought in tablets so we could listen to music, watch TV and study academics. I met a nice guy named Cartoon who said police pulled him and his friend over in a traffic stop shot his friend and then charged him for the murder. There was no Law Library access in this jail and had to rely on supervised legal requests through written correspondence. There was no coffee like there was in NY. They differentiated between civil and criminal case law and refused to provide "criminal" case when I wasn't representing myself. The Court did grant the Motion to Proceed Pro-Per I filed 2/12/18 on 1/8/19. My pro-se status was revoked on 1/16/19 after a hearing for Release O.R. Or Bail Reduction. That hearing was recorded on courtroom video cameras. The judge revoked the pro-se status after I ignored her order for a few seconds not to insist upon my innocence even though Arizona and U.S. Law require that these arguments may be presented at a bail hearing, See A.R.S. § 13-3967B(2)(4)(6); 18 U.S. Code §3142(g)(1)(2)(4). The first thing I told the judge was that I had prepared for a "two hour" hearing. She said I had "two minutes" despite the law requiring an elaborate hearing, See U.S. v. Salerno, 481 U.S. 739 (1987). They only provided civil case law because of the Civil Actions I filed while detained. Most of the useful case law I found was from huge stacks of case law that inmates would pass around or sell for a few store items. For every legal citation in this book I read ten to twenty times more law. I filed a petition for certiorari in the Supreme Court of The United States and stated I wanted to run for President, See Taebel v. Ducey et al 19-5906. I wrote to The United Nations and informed them I was a political prisoner in Arizona. I was hoping to bring media attention to my illegal detainment and I did think there was so many stupid people in government that apparently I need to be President. A convicted felon does have a right to run for any election in the country, See Franklin v. Murphy, 745 F.2d 1221 (9th Cir. 1984). I was thirty one at the time and the constitution states a person must be thirty five years of age to run for President. However, William Charles Cole Claiborne was elected to Congress at the age of twenty two and the constitution states the minimum age to be a House representative is twenty five. John Henry Eaton was elected to the senate at the age of twenty eight and the constitution states the minimum age to be a

Senator is thirty. I've never thought I would be interested in any political position other than the presidency. They should have at least reduced my bail. There was still no visitation from anyone other than a state or county approved lawyer. The food was terrible. They only brought two meals per day. In the morning it was peanut butter and bread and in the evening they brought vegetarian soy slop. Before I left they stopped serving warm dinner and started serving peanut butter and bread in the morning and for dinner on Saturday and Sunday. I'm pretty sure they messed with the food. Once I got bowl movements like a drank a whole bottle of laxatives. The conditions are in sharp contrast with rulings by the U.S. Courts, "Except for the right to come and go as he pleases, a pre-trial detainee retains all of the rights of a bailee, and his rights may not be ignored because it is expedient or economical to do so. Any restrictions and deprivations of those rights, beyond those which inhere in the confinement itself, must be justified by a compelling necessity", See Brenneman v. Madigan, 343 F. Supp. 128 (1972); See Also Jones v. Wittenberg, 509 F. Supp. 653 (1980). I once memorized three phone numbers at once challenging my memory. It was oppressive conditions. My family donates hundreds if not thousands of dollars each year to the ACLU each year who I wrote to however did nothing. It is impossible to argue that officers committing felonies on TV isn't a National Issue. There was video visitation however it is in no way a substitute for in-person visitations as they have in most jails across the Country. I spent a good amount of time talking to my cousins on the phone especially, Tim Taebel, Kerry Stoltz, Drew Eckman and Karen and Billy Czerkies. I initially lived in general population in pods of about 75 people at the 4th Avenue jail. Half the people would come out in the morning for four hours then the other half would come out in the afternoon. The groups were mixed up randomly so you didn't know if you were coming out in the morning or afternoon or who you were coming out with.

We were in cells with two people to a cell. I studied law and played cards and a little chess. Whenever I found someone who was college educated we would talk for hours. I tried to organize meetings to talk about law but the inmates were too stupid. They would all shy away from intellectual discussion. I met a guy from Michigan with a bachelors in criminal justice who killed someone with a single punch he said. We would stand around with the World Almanac and discuss the data and facts. I met a college football player from Wisconsin who got his eye gouged. He was wearing and eye patch and told me he got "jumped". Jail is Dangerous, See Smith v. Wade, 461 U.S. 30 (1983). I also met a lawyer named Mark Eric Ponsati who had been charged for killing his wife. He said he was a military prosecutor and claimed he had prosecuted and sentenced a man to death for possession of marijuana. He also said he had passed the Bar exams in six states and I was giving him legal advice. If soldiers have been executed for cannabis in the United States why did the Media act like it was unreasonable to say police should be executed for intentionally kidnapping people when the Civil Rights Act passed by our U.S. Elected representatives signed by the President says they should be? It's a crime deterrent number one and justice number two. Law enforcement are sociopaths and much worse than military who believe their defending our Liberty. A single prosecution could prevent thousands of kidnappings. They could charge them for capitol and offer a plea agreement but they aren't even charging police which essentially is giving them a green light to kidnap people. I made a number of written complaints to Donald Trump who I voted for and to the Department of Justice Civil Rights Division. They however failed to enforce the Civil Rights Act or do anything. Supreme Court law is what's called clearly established law and clearly established law means it must be respected and it is a criminal offense for state law enforcement to violate it, See 18 U.S.C. §241 & §242. Three Supreme Court rulings clearly in violation, See U.S. v. Salerno, 481 U.S. 739 (1987): Tennessee v. Garner, 471 U.S. 1 (1985); Bell v. Wolfish, 441 U.S. 520 (1979). Furthermore, the state government was clearly retaliating for my lawful exerciser of my rights. My right to free passage, my right to flee from an arrest without threat of the use of deadly force by police and my right to freedom of speech. Some people think they may have set my bail excessive in retaliation for saying on TV there was a right to resist unlawful arrest to the point of taking an officer's life if necessary and apparently no one figured out that was actually the law, See Badelk v. U.S., 177 U.S. 529 (1900). It's the law and absolutely a freedom of speech, See City of Houston, Tex. v. Hill, 482 U.S. 451 (1987). I can't possibly think of anything more appropriate to say after being kidnapped. It was one thing I wanted to make very clear before we proceeded to have further discussion. This is exactly what 18 U.S.C. §241 & §242 were designed to prevent retaliation for the lawful exercise of a person's Constitutional Rights. I sent a number of letters to the U.S Department of Justice reporting the violations of the Civil Rights Act. The federal government clearly isn't doing its job. I'll be the first to acknowledge there are good police out there but there are a lot of bad ones. Anyone who didn't have a criminal record then after turning twenty five was illegally arrested by police several times in a row should understand that there is a problem with our criminal justice system. My Youtube Channel was hacked by law enforcement without a warrant and eighteen of the twenty public videos were taken down. Or possibly youtube took them down. Either is an ethical crime and should give rise to a lawsuit. It was accessory to kidnapping and is deprivation of liberty without due process of law and a violation of the First Amendment. I have since been unable to recover my accounts because of two step verification and my new phone number When I created a new account and tried responding to Youtube comments my responses were taken down. I can't help but wonder how involved the CIA and FBI have become with the Big Tech companies and whether or not they were in any way responsible, See the documentary *The Social Dilemma* (2020). I think covid was likely released by the same law enforcement that is now probably now behind Big Tech. I eventually opted for "administrative segregation" or "protective custody" which was in the Lower Buckeye Jail. There, inmates only came out for an hour a day and with six other people. We were housed with cellmates at this location as well. I went back to general population for awhile but after a few months returned to administrative segregation. I normally prefer to be around more people but not semi-retarted dangerous inmates. I had already been in two fights that I won and didn't want to push my luck. The first was after moving into a new cell in a new house. The guy started telling me I had to leave so I asked the officer to move me. The officer was deliberately indifferent and refused to move me which is a criminal offense. Then I got attacked but I dodged most of his swings. He barely got me and I got him a couple times pretty good. Then we stopped fighting and the officers finally moved me. The second time a black guy who was in his late forties but in really good shape moved into my sell and he started pacing back and forth. Then he started getting worked up and yelling. I told him to calm down and he didn't then I grabbed him by the throat with my left hand and choked him till he stopped fighting. Then I let him go. Records show 80 people have died in the Maricopa County jail in the past decade. A lot of people are murdered in jail and I would be surprised if anyone gets charged. I also heard Alex Jones allege major election fraud from this particular county. In 2019 I missed my sisters wedding because I was unlawfully detained. I was eventually force medicated in the last year of detainment in violation of Supreme Court of The United States Law, See Sell v. U.S., 539 U.S. 166 (2003). They must have thought if they could illegally keep me detained for that long and get away with it they could get away with anything. They came in with needles and injected me with drugs twice a day for a while then changed to a time release medication once a month. I refused and they brought in a swat team with a video camera and I cited law for ten minutes telling them how illegal it was and that they could all be prosecuted. I know they were following someone else's orders which is not an exonerating argument, See the "Nuremberg Trials". This made them impossible to reason with. They threatened to drop a canister of tear gas in my cell. Medication can only be administered by force in severely ill and violent people. It was aggravated assault and torture every time. 18 U.S.C. 2340 defines torture as "acts specifically intended to inflict severe physical or mental pain or suffering". They say that medication makes permanent effects in a person's brain. I'm still healthy but no amount of damages can restore the beautiful brain I was born with and had naturally. The county has been sued and found liable for unlawfully administering drugs before, See Frost v. Agnos, 152 F.3d 1124 (9th Cir. 1998). I gained over seventy pounds and could hardly tie my shoes. I had a six pack when I was kidnapped and was benching almost 300 pounds. I Won two Film Awards in 2017. I made a Boxing video a few months before the kidnapping of me sparring with a guy bigger than I and I kicked his ass. The Film showed I was clearly of healthy body and mind. I hadn't boxed anyone is eight years. There were over ten thousand arrests of protesters following the murder of George Floyd. The corrections department seemed to have a backward philosophy. They would write people a disciplinary ticket if they refused to house with an inmate or asked to move because they feared for their safety. With legitimate safety concerns a person would still be sent to "closed custody" or disciplinary housing for one week. It doesn't make sense that people are punished for keeping themselves safe. It is unconstitutional. They write tickets because they don't want to move people around. They should just keep track of a persons requests to move and inmates who take advantage of that right can be sent to disciplinary housing or denied the move. I felt like I was being harassed the entire time. Whenever I was in a group that I got along with or had a cellmate I got along with and was in a safe location the correction officers would move me. This didn't make sense because every time you enter a new environment you risk getting attacked which should be a big liability for the jails but probably isn't. Twice, I had officers allege I had assaulted them but I was in handcuffs both times and on the other side of a door. They would allege they were scratched or injured to write up a bigger offense. The charges were declined by the County Attorneys Office both times, however the corrections department tried to have me criminally charged. Some of the guards were okay. We would talk about aliens and stuff. They were however mostly uneducated. I put a copy of my college degree in the window and to remind them I would be at least a Lieutenant if I worked there. They told me I should run for Sheriff. I tried but they wouldn't release me. I wanted to film a reality TV show about being Sheriff.

The Supreme Court of The United States ruled, "We consider whether a law enforcement official can, consistent with the Fourth Amendment, attempt to stop a fleeing motorist from continuing his public-endangering flight by ramming the motorist's car from behind.", See Scott v. Harris, 550 U.S. 372 (2007). This is what an officer did on Scottsdale Rd after exiting the highway, he rammed my vehicle in an attempt to terminate the pursuit by disabling my vehicle. In this case respondent sped away from an attempted traffic stop "exceeding 85 miles per hour" in "a 55-mile-per-hour speed limit", "colliding with Scott's police car, "force cars traveling in both directions to their respective shoulders to avoid being hit" and "running two red lights". The U.S. District court and the U.S. Court of Appeals 11th Circuit agreed that the officers use of a "Precision Intervention

Technique" known as a PIT was unlawful. The Supreme Court of The United States reversed holding the PIT was lawful under the circumstances, "The car chase that respondent initiated in this case posed a substantial and immediate risk of serious physical injury to others". Judge Steven made an epic dissent to this ruling. The video for this case can be found on The Supreme Court of The United States website and on YouTube. The video in no way reflects my slow-speed pursuit in Arizona. That was an unlawful PIT by clearly established law, See Scott v. Harris, 550 U.S. 372 (2007).

Stephen R. Wainwright a Law Student at Tulane University "left his French Quarter apartment in New Orleans to get something to eat. Approximately four blocks from his apartment, two of the New Orleans Police Department who had observed petitioner as they cruised by in their car stopped him because in their opinion he fitted the description of a man suspected of murder. That suspect had tattooed on his left forearm the words 'born to raise hell.' Petitioner told the officers he had identification at home but not on his person. He gave them his name and address, and informed them he was a law student and was on his way to get something to eat. The officers told petitioner they thought he resembled a murder suspect, and asked him to remove his jacket so they could check his forearm for the tattoo. Petitioner refused, saying he would not allow himself 'to be molested by a bunch of cops here on the street,' and he 'didn't want to be humiliated by the police.'... During this incident petitioner attempted three times peacefully to walk away from the officers... petitioner was informed he was under arrest. Evidently on the basis of this last attempt, petitioner was subsequently charged with resisting an officer... After petitioner was inside the car he called the officers 'stupid cops,' whereupon they told him he would also be charged with reviling the police... In the stationhouse... An officer then told petitioner to remove his jacket. Petitioner refused, folding his arms and crouching in a corner. Two officers, according to one of them, then 'got hold of each of his arms... and tried to pry his arms apart, and... were bounced from wall to wall and bench to bench and back again.'... Petitioner's trial for the three charges based on the episode in the street – vagrancy by loitering, resisting an officer and reviling the police – commenced... at the close of the state's case on that day petitioner's motion for dismissal was taken under advisement, and three new charges based on events inside the police station were lodged against him... Why the police waited six months before bringing charges based on events occurring within the police station is nowhere explained." I think it is obvious that the officers filed new charges in RETALIATION after his initial arrest charges were dismissed. The municipal court ruled that the arrest was lawful despite the charges being dismissed and that because petitioner was in "lawful" custody the officers had a right to book him and conduct the search. Unable to find relief in the state courts petitioner appealed to The U.S. Supreme Court where a number of judges agreed with him especially Chief Judge Warren and Douglas, See Wainwright v. City of New Orleans, 392 U.S. 598 (1968). Law Students resist unlawful arrest too.

During the night of October 3rd 1974 two Memphis police officers were dispatched to a call reporting a burglary in a neighbors home. When the officers arrived there was a woman standing on her front porch and stated she had heard glass breaking in the house next door. One officer called over the radio to confirm their arrival. The other officer went around the back of the house and saw a suspect fleeing across the yard. The officer called out, "police, halt" but the suspect did not stop. Edward Garner, the suspect, then began to climb over the fence. The officer fired and hit Garner in the back of the head. Garner died at the Hospital. "Ten dollars and a purse taken from the house were found on his body... Garner's father then brought this action in the Federal District Court for the Western District of

Tennessee, seeking damages under 42 U.S.C. 1983 for asserted violations of Garner's constitutional rights. The complaint alleged that the shooting violated the Fourth, Fifth, Sixth, Eighth and Fourteenth Amendments of the United States Constitution. It named as defendants Officer Hymon, the police Department, its Director, and the Mayor and city of Memphis. After a 3-day bench trial, the district Court entered judgment for all defendants". The Tennessee statute derived from common law stated in cases of felony "if after notice of the intention to arrest the defendant, he either flee or forcibly resists, the officer may use all the necessary means to effect the arrest". This rule originated in England common-law however at that time all felonies were punishable by death and officers did not carry hand guns. Many of the crimes now defined as felonies were at that time considered misdemeanors and the law has always prohibited the use of deadly force against a misdemeanant. "Because of sweeping change in the legal and technological context, reliance on the common-law rule in this case would be a mistaken literalism that ignores the purpose of a historical inquiry". The Court of Appeals reversed the dismissal against the city. The Supreme Court of The United States Affirmed and ruled, "We conclude that such force may not be used unless it is necessary to prevent the escape and the officer has probable cause to believe that the suspect poses a significant threat of death or serious physical injury to the officer or others". The Court also stated that, "Nor does the fact that an unarmed suspect has broken into a dwelling at night automatically mean he is dangerous". This rulings effectively saves hundreds if not thousands of lives every year. The U.S. Supreme Court affirmed the right of a nonviolent felon or misdemeanant to flee from arrest without the threat of deadly force being used against him or her, See Tennessee v. Garner, 471 U.S. 1 (1985): See also Orn v. City of Tacoma, 949 F.3d 1167 (9th Cir. 2020).

All states are bound to U.S. Supreme Court rulings and if state law conflicts it is invalidated, See Mutual Pharmaceutical Co., Inc. v. Bartlett, 570 U.S. 472 (2013). "This Constitution, and the Laws of the United States which shall be made in Pursuance thereof; and all Treaties made, or which shall be made, under the Authority of the United States, shall be the Supreme Law of the Land; and the Judges in every State shall be bound thereby, any Thing in the Constitution or Laws of any State to the Contrary notwithstanding.", See Article VI §2. This is known as The Supremacy Clause. The U.S. Supreme Court can overrule Congressional Acts or Executive Orders, See Marbury v Madison, 5 U.S. 137 (1803); U.S. v. Nixon, 418 U.S. 683 (1974). The Supreme Court of The United States is the law of the land however it's authority still comes second to the Constitution itself and the Declaration of Independence. I made sure to put a lot of U.S. Supreme Court law in this book to make sure reading it is time well spent. The U.S. Supreme Court has overruled over one hundred Congressional acts and thousands of state laws. It is a major issue in this country that lower courts especially state courts don't follow U.S. Supreme Court law. The states in their masses as if rebelling against the rule of law and the Supreme Court of the United States are arbitrary. Discrepancies between Supreme Court law and the practices of state district courts are often left for the appellate courts who likely offer no revise.

Excessive Force may invalidate an otherwise lawful arrest. "Convictions cannot be brought about by methods that offend a sense of justice.", See Rochin v. California, 342 U.S. 165 (1952); See also Smith v. City of Hemet, 394 F.3d 689 (9th Cir. 2005). Judge Douglas of The U.S. Supreme Court affirmed that excessive force may invalidate an arrest stating, "The Ohio Supreme Court sustained the conviction even though it was based on the documents obtained in the lawless search. For in Ohio evidence obtained by an unlawful search and seizure is admissible in a criminal prosecution at least where it was not taken from the defendant's person by the use of brutal or offensive force against defendant.", See Mapp v. Ohio, 367 U.S. 643 (1961) (Douglas). This makes sense because the 4th Amendment literally protects every citizen from "unreasonable searches and seizures" and an arrest is a seizure, See Brower v. County of Inyo, 489 U.S. 593 (1989); Graham v. Connor, 490 U.S. 386 (1989). The unlawful arrest in Arizona was an "unreasonable seizure" in violation of the fruit-of-the-poisonous-tree doctrine and barred from use in any state court, See Mapp v. Ohio, 367 U.S. 643 (1961). Article II of the 1998 European Human Rights Act states an officer making an arrest may not use force that is more than "absolutely necessary".

The supreme Court of The United States overturned a conviction in a case where the petitioners had record showing "a total of 54 previous arrests", the court ruled, "the conviction is not supported by evidence, in which event it does not comport with due process of law.", See Thompson v. City of Louisville, 362 U.S. 199 (1960). The Court later stated, "a properly instructed jury may occasionally convict even when it can be said that no rational trier of fact could find guilt beyond a reasonable doubt, and the same may be said of a trial judge sitting as a jury" and in regards to vacating a conviction ruled, "the relevant question is whether, after viewing the evidence in the light most favorable to the prosecution, any rational trier of fact could have found the essential elements of the crime beyond a reasonable doubt.", See Jackson v. Virginia, 443 U.S. 307 (1979). I"m absolutely positive that no rational trier of fact could find proof beyond a reasonable doubt in my NYC Self-Defense case, therefore that conviction must be overturned.

Judge Harlan of The Supreme Court of The United States stated in concurring opinion, "I view the requirement of proof beyond a reasonable doubt in a criminal case as bottomed on a fundamental value determination of our society that it is far worse to convict an innocent man than to let a guilty man go free.". The Court stated in majority opinion, "use of the reasonable-doubt standard is indispensable to command the respect and confidence of the community in applications of the criminal law. It is critical that the moral force of the criminal law not be diluted by a standard of proof that leaves people in doubt whether innocent men are being condemned. It is also important in our free society that every individual going about his ordinary affairs have confidence that his government cannot adjudge him guilty of a criminal offense without convincing a proper factfinder of his guilt with utmost certainty" and ruled, "We explicitly hold that the Due Process Clause protects the accused against conviction except upon proof beyond a reasonable doubt of every fact necessary to constitute the crime with which he is charged.", See In re Winship, 397 U.S. 358 (1970). The U.S. Supreme Court ruled a few years later in unanimous decision, that a government must prove proof beyond a reasonable doubt, the absence of self-defense, See Mullaney v. Wilbur, 421 U.S. 684 (1975). Self-defense is a justification defense, "If evidence of justification pursuant to chapter 4 of this title is presented by the defendant, the state must prove beyond a reasonable doubt that the defendant did not act with justification.", See A.R.S. 13-205A. "It is far better that ten guilty persons escape, than one innocent suffer."= William Blackstone.

In order to lawfully convict a person the evidence must show at least a 99% probability of Guilt. That standard is arguably low. At 99% one person out of one hundred people would be innocent. There are over 10,000,000 arrests each year. That would mean at least 100,000 would be unjustly prosecuted and could face imprisonment. That is enough to make any person with a conscious sick.

The unconstitutional conviction in NYC is 150,000% against the weight of the evidence. Here is a breakdown of the evidence with proportional values given to each piece of evidence:

Defense:	Prosecution:
Video +5	
Police Reports +3	
Medical Reports +3	
Indictment Transcripts +3	
Second Witness +1	
My Testimony +5	Complaining Witness +1

Total:	20	1

That's 2,000% against the weight of the evidence as to who was at fault. To the standard of proof beyond a reasonable doubt that's about 200,000% against the weight of the evidence.

In Arizona here is my breakdown of the Evidence:

Defense: **Prosecution:**

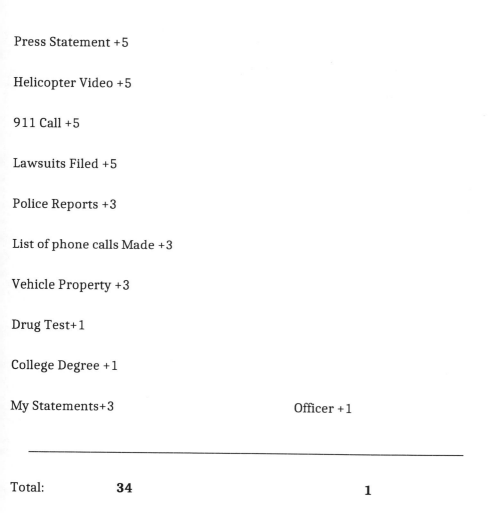

Press Statement +5

Helicopter Video +5

911 Call +5

Lawsuits Filed +5

Police Reports +3

List of phone calls Made +3

Vehicle Property +3

Drug Test+1

College Degree +1

My Statements+3   Officer +1

_____

Total: **34**   **1**

Thats 3,400% against the weight of the evidence as to who is at fault. To the standard of proof beyond a reasonable doubt that's about 340,000% against the weight of the evidence.

    The chances of a college graduate being guilty of any of the things I was charged with are probably less than 1/10,000. Only about 30% of the U.S.

population has a college degree while less than 1/1000 of inmates are degree holders. Out of thousands of people, I met only three men with degrees while in Phoenix. Two of which were in there for killing their wives and the other was there for a self-defense homicide. Those with a degree statistically earn about twice as much as those without, See Bureau of Labor Statistics, U.S. Department of Labor. Which is one reason they tend to stay out of jail. Two of three inmates in Arizona can't read and write above a 7th grade level, See Casey v. Lewis, 43 F.3d 1261 (9th Cir. 1994). Those with a degree earn about three times as much as those without a high school diploma. About nine of ten inmates dropped out of high school. In 2000 less than 60% of high school students in Arizona actually graduate, See National Center for Education Statistics, U.S. Department of Education. As a College graduate I should have been entitled to very reasonable bail. Furthermore most of Hollywood does not have college degrees. Many of them dropped out of High school which proves you don't have to have any formal education to be an intellectual.

CHAPTER 6

The U.S. Supreme Court ruled on a case where a state judge was convicted under 18 U.S.C. §242 for seven counts of sexual assault and sentenced to consecutive maximum terms totaling 25 years! The allegations are as follows "while Lanier was in office, he sexually assaulted several women in his judicial chambers. The two most serious assaults were against women whose divorce proceedings had come before Lanier and whose daughter's custody remained subject to his jurisdiction. When the woman applied for a secretarial job at Lanier's courthouse, Lanier interviewed her and suggested that he might have to reexamine the daughter's custody. When the woman got up to leave, Lanier grabbed her, sexually assaulted her, and finally committed oral rape. A few weeks later, Lanier inveigled the woman into returning to the courthouse again to get information about another job opportunity, and again sexually assaulted and orally raped her. On five other occasions Lanier sexually assaulted four other women... Ultimately, Lanier was charged with 11 violations of §242, each count of the indictment alleging that, acting willfully and under color of Tennessee law, he had deprived the victim of 'rights and privileges which are secured and protected by the constitution and the laws of the united states, namely the right not to be deprived of liberty without due process of law, including the right to be free from wilful sexual assault.' Before trial Lanier moved to dismiss the indictment on the ground that §242 is void for vagueness. The District Court Denied the Motion." The U.S. Court of Appeals "On rehearing, the Court set aside Lanier's convictions for 'lack of any notice to the public that this ambiguous criminal statute included simple or sexual assault crimes within its coverage.'" The U.S. Supreme Court remanded in unanimous decision for good reason. However it is impossible to prove beyond a reasonable doubt that it was not consensual if she returned to the courthouse and didn't make a report of it for weeks. Lanier should bring a claim under Thompson v. City of Louisville, 362 U.S. 199 (1960) and prevail against at least some of the charges. It does not indicate that he ever attempted that argument. A victim of a crime has a duty to make a report of it as soon as possible or the justification for prosecution rapidly declines. It doesn't sound as though she immediately made a report of it but it does not say. The risk of an unjustified prosecution increases and the crime of unjustly sentencing a man to years in prison is worse than any of the allegations against him. If a woman intends to charge a man for rape she needs to physically fight and scream. Lanier received two ten year sentences for licking a woman's pussy on TWO OCASSIONS who went back to see him from what is in the ruling it sounds as if she didn't put up much resistance or even make an initial report of it.

The United States has the highest incarceration rate in the world according to the U.N. Survey on crime trends and operations of criminal justice systems. Our prisoner rates are over five times higher than China. This means we have a problem. Corporations through government contracts have turned imprisonment into a business, leasing the facilities, equipment and services to state and federal governments. Private prisons should be ruled unconstitutional. Our Incarceration rate is over ten times higher than most modern world countries. The Supreme Court ruled "deprivations of liberty that go hand in hand with criminal prosecutions.", See Manuel v. City of Joliet, Ill., 580 S. Ct. 911 (2017); quoting Albright v. Oliver, 510 U.S 266 (1994). Corrections Corporation of America is the nations largest owner of private prisons in the U.S. and their profits are ever increasing even when crime rates are declining. Many of these government contracts usually require the states to keep their prisons filled near maximum capacity. Arizona has three prison contracts requiring 100% capacity which is the highest in the country. It doesn't make sense for the government to use tax money to pay private for profit corporations to manage their jails and prisons. These facilities should be publicly owned and operated. Article I §9 of the U.S. Constitution states: "The privilege of the writ of Habeas Corpus shall not be suspended, unless when in Cases of Rebellion or invasion the public Safety may require it". The writ of Habeas Corpus is a civil action against unlawful detainment. This was one of the only explicit protections declared in the central constitution before the Bill of Rights were ratified because the framers were already very familiar with governments tendencies exceed its lawful authority and detain people unlawfully. Law enforcement promotes crime to justify their job and more money. I can tell you after my experience in NYC and Arizona that they give affirmation to the criminal philosophy. For instance if two guys steal your stuff in jail and you report it, you get moved out of the house and the two thieves stay there and probably don't even get tickets. Common sense would dictate that the person who reports theft stays in his cell and house while the thieves get taken to disciplinary housing after getting tickets. They also should be criminally charged in cases of theft or assault in a better effort to discourage criminal conduct and the mentality. You can't create an environment where it makes sense to think and act like a criminal. That is clearly counterproductive to the tax payer's dollars and promotes criminal behavior. The most effective crime prevention comes from instilling proper values in the community through school, church, respectable law enforcement, ect... Detention facilities and prisons should use resources to support proper values and provide avenues for employment and vocational training. I once heard an African-American detention officer say white people were a "dying race". At least that's not true if you consider Latinos white people like Charles Murray, See FACING REALITY: Two Truths about Race in America, Encounter Books, New York (2021). Most of the guards in NYC were African-American. I can tell you that tax dollars are being spent on a corrections department that believe in black power and evil. I remember hearing a black inmate say he was just "invading these crackers" as if it was his purpose in life. These places are factories of insolence. In Phoenix most of the detention officers were white and Latino. Neither of the jails were rehabilitative in any way.

In 1964 twenty one officers were arrested for murder after three Civil Rights Workers were kidnapped and found dead in Mississippi. The allegations were that the three men had been detained in the Neshoba County jail and then released in the dark of night. The three men were traveling by automobile when they were intercepted by law enforcement who make a traffic stop then removed from their vehicle. They were placed in a law enforcement vehicle and taken down an unpaved road where they were then killed by a number of officers including the sheriff and deputy sheriff. Seven of the defendants were convicted under the Civil Rights Act 18 U.S.C. §242 the Act I cited on TV. The case went to the Supreme Court of The United States who remanded for prosecution, See U.S. v. Price, 383 U.S. 787 (1966); See The Movie *Mississippi Burning* (1988) nominated for seven Oscars and winner of an Academy Award. Thirty years later Byron De La Beckwith was convicted for his involvement with the murders.

Mens Rea is Latin for "guilty mind" and must be proven beyond a reasonable doubt in order for a prosecution to obtain a criminal conviction, See Staples v. United States, 511 U.S. 600 (1994); See also Morisette v. United States, 342 U.S. 246 (1952). Mens rea is also known as criminal intent. A person must have intended to commit the crime in order to be convicted. All my arrests are clearly absent mens rea. For example when I acted in self-defense in NYC I was consciously acting according to law because I had studied the principles of self=defense in college. This means I intended not to act unlawfully but rather within my rights as defined by law. There was no mens rea, I didn't make up the claim of self-defense after the incident, I was already very familiar with the principles. It was what's called a "perfect self-defense". The refusal to stop for an officer in phoenix, similarly, was for lawful reasons and absent mens rea. Even if they attempt to argue the stop or arrest was legal they cannot deny the fact that my actions were for lawful reasons because I clearly stated that in the 911 call and to the police immediately after the unlawful arrest. The requirement of "mens rea" to obtain a conviction for most criminal offenses is the practice across Europe as well, See Jonathan Herring, *Criminal Law 10th Edition*, London, Palgrave Law Masters, Published 2017.

In one of the greatest U.S. Supreme Court cases on Freedom of Speech, "Appellee Raymond Wayne Hill is a lifelong resident of Houston, Texas. At the time this lawsuit began, he worked as a paralegal and executive director of the Houston Human Rights League. A member of the board of the Gay Political Caucus, which he helped found in 1975, Hill was also affiliated with the Houston radio station, and had carried city and county press passes since 1975.". On February 14th 1982, Hill watched two police officers approach his friend who had stopped traffic on a busy street in order to allow a vehicle to enter traffic. Hill began shouting at the officer in an admitted attempt to divert the officer's attention from his friend. Hill shouted, "Why don't you pick on somebody your own size?" The officer then responded and asked Hill if he was interrupting him in his official duties. Hill than shouted again, "Why don't you pick on somebody your own size?" The officer then arrested Hill under an ordinance that read, "It shall be unlawful for any person to assault, strike or in other manner oppose, molest, abuse or interrupt any policeman in the execution of his duty, or any person summoned to aid in making an arrest." The ordinance, "under which he has been arrested four times since 1975, but never convicted." was then challenged in The U.S. District Court which dismissed his claim. The Court of Appeals however reversed. The Supreme Court of The United States affirmed invalidating the ordinance on 1st Amendment grounds and ruled, "Today's decision reflects the constitutional requirement that, in the face of verbal challenges to police action, officers and municipalities must respond with restraint.", See City of Houston, Tex. v. Hill, 482 U.S. 451 (1987). The court then stated in the footnotes, "We therefore agree with the Court of Appeals that 'Hill's record of arrests under the ordinance and his adopted role as citizen provocateur' give Hill standing to challenge the facial validity of the ordinance.", (Fn.7). The Court also described his previous three arrests: "The facts of Hill's other three arrests as found by the District Court are as follows. On August 31,1975, Hill intentionally interrupted two Houston police officers as they made a traffic arrest. During the arrest, Hill wrote down license plate numbers, and the walked to within an arm's length of one of the officers on the side nearest the officer's revolver. The officer asked Hill to leave, but Hill instead moved closer. Hill was arrested, tried, and found not guilty. In 1977, after observing vice-squad cars parked near a bookstore, Hill entered the store and announced on the public address system that police officers were present and that patrons should prepare to show their identification. The patrons promptly left the store, thereby frustrating the investigation. Hill was arrested for interfering with the investigation, but the case subsequently dismissed. Finally, on October 3rd, 1982, eight months after the lawsuit began, Hill was arrested for refusing to leave the immediate area of a car with an unknown and unconscious person inside. The arresting officers failed to appear in Municipal Court, however, so the charge against Hill was dismissed.", See City of Houston, Tex. v. Hill, 482 U.S. 451 (1987)(Fn.4).

Police are required to have a warrant to make an arrest for a misdemeanor not committed in their presence from coast to coast, See Florida: Johnson v. Barnes & Noble Booksellers Inc.,437 F.3d 1112 (11th Cir. 2006); See California: Arpin v. Santa Clara Valley Transp. Agency, 261 F.3d 912 (9th Cir. 2001); See New York: U.S. v. Di Re, 332 U.S. 581 (1948); See Oregon: Bergstrath v. Lowe, 504 F.2d 1276 (9th Cir. 1974). The "in-presence rule" is defined as "The principle that a police officer may make a warrantless arrest of a person who commits a misdemeanor offense not only in the officer's actual presence but also within the officer's immediate vicinity", See Black's Law Dictionary, West Publishing Co. (2016). This practice is to protect the public from careless or impulsive arrests however police lobbying threatens this standard in some areas in this country like NYC. My arrest in NYC was for a misdemeanor without a warrant, not committed in an officers presence, that was indicted over nine months after the unlawful arrest. Most states have explicit legislation affirming this traditional protection. "In cases of misdemeanors, a peace officer like a private person has at common law no power of arresting without a warrant except when a breach of the peace has been committed in his presence or there is reasonable ground for supposing that a breach of peace is about to be committed or renewed in his presence.", Carroll v. United States, 267 U.S. 132 (1925); quoting Halsbury, Law of England §612, p.299 (1909); See also William A. Schroeder, *Warrantless Misdemeanor Arrests and the Fourth Amendment,* 58 MO. L. REV. (1993).

Amendment IV of The U.S. Constitution states: "The right of the people to be secure in their persons, houses, papers, and effects, against unreasonable searches and seizures, shall not be violated, and no warrants shall issue, but upon probable cause, supported by oath or affirmation, and particularly describing the place to be searched, and the persons or things to be seized." Many of the problems we see today are due to illegal searches and seizures, "Among deprivations of rights, none is so effective in cowing a population, crushing the spirit of the individual and putting terror in every heart. Uncontrolled search and seizure is one of the first and most effective weapons in the arsenal of every arbitrary government.", See Almeida-Sanchez v. United States, 413 U.S. 266 (1973). The law in England since before this country was founded was that officer needs probable cause to make an arrest. This means that they must have compelling evidence that someone has or is about to commit a crime. There must be a probability of a person's guilt. A single witness without supporting evidence isn't enough to sustain probable cause, See Jones v. U.S., 362 U.S. 257 (1960); See also Florida v. J.L., 529 U.S. 266 (2000). The government shouldn't have thought they had probable cause to make an arrest and especially not after I called 911 and informed them I wasn't stopping because I had just filed lawsuits in court against kidnappings and the attempted traffic stop was illegal. This was a case of two conflicting witnesses between me and a single officer. The Arizona Jury instructions explicitly state "The testimony of a Law enforcement officer is not entitled to any greater or lesser importance or believability merely because of the fact that the witness is a law enforcement officer. You are to consider the testimony of a police officer just as you would the testimony of any other witness.", See Testimony of Law Enforcement Officers. This means that two conflicting witnesses alone is factually impossible to prove anything beyond a reasonable doubt and I had a lot of evidence on my side. That's not probable cause. The state never had a legitimate case against me. For another example, if officers responds to a call for domestic disturbance because two people are arguing and one of them claims the other threatened them with a knife, the officers wont have probable cause if the other person denies it, absent some other forms of supporting evidence. This is known as "he/she said". Two conflicting testimonies alone cannot sustain probable cause. In cases of uncorroborated allegations of domestic violence the woman should leave. Police shouldn't make arrests without proof of injury. The "two-witness rule" is defined as, "The doctrine that a federal prosecution requires proof either by two witnesses or by one witness whose testimony is corroborated by other evidence.", See *Black's Law Dictionary* (2016). "If it is a requirement of due process for a trial in the federal courthouse, it is impossible for me to say it is not a requirement of due process for a trial in the state courthouse.", See Rochin v. California, 342 U.S. 165 (1952)(Douglas). Article III §3 of The U.S. Constitution states: "No person shall be convicted of Treason unless on the Testimony of two witnesses to the same overt Act, or on confession in open Court". Although there are only a few crimes mentioned in the Constitution all crimes should require about the same standard of proof. "We note the applicability of Justice POWELL's observation that there is a 'possibility of abuse' where convictions under an ordinance frequently turn on the resolution of a 'direct conflict of testimony as to 'who said what.' Lewis v. City of New Orleans, 415 U.S. 130...(1974)(Powell,J., concurring in result)", See City of Houston, Tex. v. Hill, 482 U.S. 451 (1987) (Fn.2). The standard for both probable cause and proof beyond a reasonable doubt are eroding and the result is a tyrannical government that is prosecuting the innocent on a single uncorroborated and often false testimony. Just as an officer must have probable cause to make an arrest, and often required to have a warrant, police must also have probable cause and are often required to have a warrant for a search. Evidence unconstitutionally obtained is not permitted to be used in a criminal prosecution. This is known as the "fruit-of-the-poisonous-tree doctrine" which is defined as "The rule that evidence derived from an illegal search, arrest, or interrogation is inadmissible because the evidence (the 'fruit') was tainted by the illegality (the 'poisonous tree')", See Black's Law Dictionary, West Publishing Co. (2016). The use of excessive force in Arizona constituted a violation of this doctrine. An affidavit in support of a complaint or a warrant must contain detailed facts to support probable cause, See Spinelli v. U.S., 393 U.S. 410 (1969). The U.S. Supreme Court has also ruled, "when a search is based upon a magistrate's, rather than a police officer's determination of probable cause, the reviewing courts will accept evidence of a less judicially competent or persuasive character than would have justified an officer in acting on his own without a warrant", See Aguilar v. State of Tex., 378 U.S. 108 (1964). A standard for evaluating an affidavit has been comprised of these two cases and is known as the Aguilar-Spinelli test. Neither the arrest in Manhattan or Arizona were supported by probable Cause.

Amendment VIII of the U.S. Constitution states: "Excessive bail shall not be required". This has been ruled by The Supreme Court of The United States to imply a right to release after an arrest, See U.S. v. Salerno, 481 U.S. 739 (1987) (w/Dissents). This is because the paramount value of the presumption of innocence and due process of law. "And upon all arrests in criminal cases, bail shall be admitted, except where the punishment may be death", See First Congress Ch. XX §33. Nowadays even those charged with a capitol offense may be entitled to bail. The biggest difference between a kidnapping by police and an arrest is the practice of releasing a defendant on reasonable bail. "The plain meaning of "excessive bail" does not require that it be beyond one's means, only that it be greater than necessary to achieve the purposes for which bail is imposed.", See Galen v. County of Los Angeles, 477 F.3d 652 (9th Cir. 2007). The English Bill of Rights in 1689 stated "excessive bail ought not to be required". In 1984 Congress passed The Bail Reform Act 18 U.S. Code §3142. The States are bound to the regulations of this act. Section C(2) clearly states "The judicial officer may not impose a financial condition that results in the pretrial detention of the person." In 2014 The U.S. 9th Circuit ruled in a case where nine of eleven judged ruled in Concurrence including the Chief Judge, the court stated there is a "general rule of substantive due process that the government may not detain a person prior to a judgment of guilt in a criminal trial.", See Lopez-Valenzuela v. Arpaio, 770 F.3d 772 (2014); See also Melendres v. Arpaio, 784 F. 3d 1254 (9th Cir. 2015) . Joe Arpaio, the previous Sheriff for Maricopa County was criminally convicted for violating this court order July 31st 2017, less than six months before my unlawful arrest in phoenix however he was Pardoned by Trump. Despite the criminal conviction of Arpaio they showed complete disregard for the law in my case because I was detained for over three years on a $400,000 "cash only" bail. The Congressional Bail Reform act requires a state to give and adversary detention hearing if a person is not immediately released, "The person shall be afforded an opportunity to testify, to present witnesses, to cross-examine witnesses who appear at the hearing, and to present information by proffer or otherwise" and "The hearing shall be held immediately upon the person's first appearance before the judicial officer unless that person, or the attorney for the Government, seeks a continuance. Except for good cause, a continuance on motion of such person may not exceed five days", See 18 U.S.C. §3142 (f) (2) (B). In other words the accused has the absolute right to present evidence showing their detainment is unjustified. A rule which Arizona did not comply with. The U.S. Ninth Circuit Court order mandated compliance with the Congressional Bail Reform Act. County Attorney william g. montgomery was also a respondent in that court order and should have been prosecuted as well. He supervises all the prosecutions in the county. He should be prosecuted for my detainment and malicious prosecution, See 18 U.S.C. §371; 18 U.S.C. §1201; 18 U.S.C. §241 & §242. As should the other respondents in my law suits like governor douglas ducey. I read through hundreds of inmates paperwork and I had by far the most prejudicial and excessive bail. Even Arizona Law says I should have been released "on his own recognizance or on the execution of bail", See A.R.S. § 13-3967 (A). The Arizona Constitution requires that everyone charged with a crime be released on reasonable bail, See In re Haigler, 15 Ariz. 150 (1930); Ariz. Const. Art. II §15 and §22. "The amount of $50,000 could have no other purpose than to make it impossible for him to give the bail and to detain him in custody, and is unreasonable. The Constitutional right to be admitted to reasonable bail cannot be disregarded. The judge has no more right to disregard and violate the constitution than the criminal has to violate the law.", See People ex rel. Sammons v Snow, 349 Ill. 464 (1930). There is one case which represents my detainment particularly well, See Wagenmann v. Adams, 829 F.2d 196 (1st Cir. 1987); See Also Gonzalez v. Bratton, 147 F. Supp. 2d 180 (S.D.N.Y. 2001).

The media has a right to attend pretrial hearings in most cases, See Waller v. Georgia, 467 U.S. 39 (1984). However, the "unconstitutional" media preclusion order either directly prevented them from doing so or turned the media away enough that they chose not to attend, See Nebraska Press Association v. Stuart, 427 US 539 (1976). The illegal preclusion order was filed for by my private attorney who I had already fired over the phone, however, remained on the case until he received a written letter of termination. The media has a right to cover Courtrooms across Europe. Article VI §1.7.2(c) of the 1998 European Human Rights Act states the media and public may only be excluded from the courtroom "in the interest of morals, public order or national security, where the interest of juveniles or the private life of the parties so require, or to the extent strictly necessary in the opinion of the court". In the Phoenix case the issues the media should have been concerned with should have been heard in pretrial hearings: entrapment, probable cause, unreasonable seizure, lack of mens rea, suppression of the traffic stop, ect.. I would have liked to see the press at every hearing covering the story.

The private attorney retained in Arizona for $10,000 did everything I didn't want him to do and nothing I wanted him to. Instead of making a valid defense by arguing absence of mens rea, self-defense, entrapment and lack of probable cause he apparently claimed I had mental health issues to the press, See Tower v. Glover, 467 U.S. 914 (1984). He should have blamed the police for their use of excessive force and called it entrapment. I had only one meeting with him the day after the News conference where I informed him that my highest priority was to get released on bail. I asked him to bring back the police reports as soon as possible. It was my experience in other states that lawyers retained for a pre-arraignment investigation would provide the police reports within hours of the arrest. When he didn't return with the reports, I fired him over the telephone a few days later. He then proceeded to file a motion requesting a media preclusion order which the court granted. He also filed a motion requesting a rule 11 or competency evaluation which the court granted. The insanity defense may have worked for John Hinckley Jr. who shot and wounded Ronald Reagan, however I had no intentions of making an insanity defense because I already had a very legitimate defense. The incompetence to stand trial defense should not have applied to me, I do not in any way reflect the criminal defendants it usually applies to, See Jackson v. Indiana, 406 U.S. 715 (1972); Pate v. Robinson, 383 U.S. 375 (1966). The attorney took it upon himself, without my consent, to motion for a media preclusion order and to make an incompetence to stand trial defense, See Tower v. Glover, 467 U.S. 914 (1984). Arizona Rules of Professional Conduct Rule 1.2 (Scope of Representation and Allocation of Authority between Client and Lawyer) states "a lawyer shall abide by a client's decisions concerning the objectives of representation and, as required by ER 1.4, shall consult with the client as to the means by which they are to be pursued. A lawyer may take such action on behalf of the client as is impliedly authorized to carry out the representation". The motions the private attorney filed were not "impliedly authorized" nor did the lawyer consult with me as to the "means"of the defense. Because of the rule 11 proceedings I was detained for over three years. The courts never gave me a chance to make another defense, they wouldn't hear any arguments. I would file them on record but they wouldn't respond or compel the prosecutor to respond. This is the kind of lawless totalitarian government we're dealing with, that detain people without hearings or due process. A Hearing is a basic requirement of due process before a person is deprived of any kind of property, See Haines v. Kerner, 404 U.S. 519 (1972); Sniadach v. Family Finance Corporation of Bay View, 395 U.S. 337 (1969); Goldberg v. Kelly, 397 U.S. 254 (1970); Goss v. Lopez, 419 U.S. 565 (1975). Why couldn't I get a hearing on my detainment, it's required by law, See U.S. v. Salerno, 481 U.S. 739 (1987). Any respectable man would find this kind of conduct by a lawyer, by the courts and by the police absolutely unacceptable. I made a State Bar complaint against the lawyer and filled a federal complaint against him alleging accessory to kidnapping. They however, at this time, have failed to take disciplinary action. I find it wholly apparent that the intentions of the lawyer and the police were to discredit me and keep me off TV, See Wagenmann v. Adams, 829 F.2d 196 (1st Cir. 1987).

The Supreme Court of The United States ruled on a case where a criminal defendant charged with grand theft was not permitted to represent himself through his trial. The California Court of Appeals affirmed and The Supreme Court denied review. The defendant then brought a petition for certiorari in The Supreme Court of The United States and the court reversed his conviction stating, "The right to the assistance of counsel, the court concluded, was intended to supplement the other rights of the defendant, and not to impair the absolute and primary right to conduct one's own defense in propria persona.". The Court also stated, "An unwanted counsel 'represents' the defendant only through a tenuous and unacceptable legal fiction. Unless the accused has acquiesced in such representation, the defense presented is not the defense guaranteed him by the Constitution, for, in a very real sense, it is not his defense.", See Faretta v. California, 422 U.S. 806 (1975). The right to self-representation can also be found in 28 U.S.C. §1654. It was an explicit right in the Judiciary Act of 1789 and was signed by President George Washington, See First Congress, Chapter XX Section 35. Many states prior to 1963 required defendants in most cases to represent themselves, See Gideon v. Wainwright, 372 U.S. 335 (1963). The occasional pro-se defendant is good for the legal system. It should be considered a respectable thing to make one's own defense, especially in cases of false arrest. I represented my own defense twice in California and was 100% successful both times. It does not do the legal system any good to take a plea agreement if a person was in fact arrested without probable cause. None of my state appointed attorneys made any effort to make a legitimate defense or get the bail reduced. They all essentially acquiesced to the fraudulent competency proceedings that had been initiated by the original private attorney I fired. The arguments of unlawful arrest need to be presented to the court but never were formerly. In some cases a defendant may feel they have no choice because a public defender may have their own legal strategy or may not be willing to make a legitimate defense at all, See Tower v. Glover, 467 U.S. 914 (1984).

CHAPTER 7

Ronald E. Wagenmann who is "a resident of New York City, is a former NYC police officer, a one-time fire fighter" went to see his daughter in Worcester, Massachusetts four days before her wedding. "At trial, Wagenmann explained that his religious convictions could not allow him to accept the kind of premarital trysting which had sprung up between Linda and Stephen" (his daughter and her fiance). Wagenmann warned that he would come to Worcester "if access to his daughter was thwarted". Stephen responded by making the following threat: "If you come to Worcester, I'll have you arrested... My father is a powerful man in Worcester...". Wagenmann wanted to "see Linda on the eve of her wedding, present with a her with a gift, and attempt to reconcile the differences which had divided them", he later testified. His wife Yvonne called ahead to warn her daughter Linda of her father's surprise visit. First Wagenmann went to Linda's office however she wasn't there. Then Wagenmann went to his daughters apartment in Brighton where he was greeted by her roommate Debbie Walsh. Although she knew where Linda was she pretended as if she didn't know. Wagenmann then left agreeing to call her apartment at 10:00pm. However at that time she still hadn't returned. Debbie Walsh then called Stephen Anderson's home "expressing concern that Wagenmann might be on his way to Worcester... the story circulated—with Anderson's help—that Wagenmann was en route to Worcester with homicide on his mind". Anderson looked up the Deputy Police Chief's phone number in the phone book and called him reporting the rumors and requested police protection. Egan dispatched Lieutenant William O'Leary to investigate. Egan and O'Leary both, later testified that Wagenmann was not supposed to be arrested on the basis of Anderson's allegations alone. O'Leary dispatched officer Pozzi to visit the Anderson's home to investigate. Afterwards, "Pozzi spotted his car and called for assistance. Within minutes, a battery of police cruisers converged and brought the vehicle to a stop. Wagenman was ordered to disembark and was promptly handcuffed... Then, although Wagenmann was never asked to produce license or registration, Pozzi issued a citation (marked 'complaint') which charged him with driving without a valid operator's license or registration". When plaintiff objected, Pozzi stated: "You understand, we just can't let you go". When Wagenman asked to arrange bail, Pozzi responded, "You have $480 and the bail is $500". In court, Pozzi then recommended to the judge that "appellee be committed for psychiatric examination... Thereafter, Wagenmann was examined at the court's initiative by a psychiatrist, Dr. David Myerson. Forewarned to expect a bellicose individual, the physician instead found plaintiff to be 'a very pleasant man, cooperative, intelligent, denying everything in any way that could question him, showing no signs of mental illness whatsoever.' In Dr. myerson's view, 'he was clearly competent.'... The psychiatrist reported these findings. He was then confronted by judge Luby, who maintained that Wagenmann was dangerous and homicidal. Myerson protested, but in vain; the judge told him that, if Wagenmann went out and did anything, he would be held responsible. It was under this sort of duress that Myerson reluctantly agreed to sign a form stating the opinion that the plaintiff should be admitted to the hospital for observation". "During the first meeting. Healy introduced himself as a court-appointed attorney. As Wagenmann recalled it, Healy never inquired as to what happened, but did say that he was a friend and fellow parishioner of Anderson's. Wagenmann, taken back, told Healy to get him another lawyer. Healy refused... he informed his client that 'the deal is that you have to commit yourself to the mental hospital.'... Healy advised Wagenmann, 'maybe in New York you're something, but up here, you're nothing'. Healy then walked away... Wagenmann was thereafter informed by his counsel that—without any personal appearance before Judge Luby--he had been committed to a mental hospital for a twenty day observation period... Wagenmann was then confined to Worcester State Hospital (WSH)... When he first arrived at WSH, Wagenmann had been interviewed by Dr. Lorenz, a psychiatrist. The examiner found no cause for commitment. Lorenz told him that 'the only reason you are being committed is because of this court order'. The next morning, he was visited by Dr. Myerson, three other psychiatrists, and a WSH staff member. Myerson, apologizing profusely for what had happened, then called Chief Judge Gould of the state district court. It was Judge Gould, who after this discussion, arranged for Wagenmann's immediate release on personal recognizance. The appellee, free at last, reclaimed his personal belongings (including $480 in cash) and boarded a bus bound for New York. Shortly thereafter, Judge Gould dismissed all three pending criminal complaints against Wagenmann". "Wagenmann's federal cause of action under 42 U.S.C. Sec. 1983 stemmed from alleged false arrest, excessive bail, and unlawful commitment to a mental institution... After six days of courtroom combat, each of the present appellants--Anderson, Healy, officer Francis J. Pozzi, and Lt. Paul Campbell—moved for direct verdicts on all accounts. So did the defendant Daniel Egan, Worcester's deputy chief of police. The district court denied these motions... On July 18, 1985, verdicts were returned in favor of the plaintiff on his federal civil rights claims for false arrest, excessive bail, and unlawful commitment, and on his tort claims for false imprisonment, intentional infliction of emotional distress, and legal malpractice... And, in connection with the civil rights claims generally, they tagged Anderson, Pozzi, and Campbell with punitive damages in the amounts of $50,000, $25,000, and $10,000, respectively. Last but not least, a $5000,000 malpractice verdict was rendered against Healy... Following the verdicts, which aggregated some $1,6000,000 in compensatory damages and $85,000 in exemplary damages", See Wagenmann v. Adams, 829 F.2d 196 (1st Cir. 1987).

Attorneys especially public defenders often have conflicts of interest, do not provide effective assistance of counsel, and sometimes conspire against their clients. Justice O'Connor delivered the opinion of the unanimous court, "Petitioners are two public defenders working in the state of Oregon. Petitioner Bruce Tower, the Douglas County Public Defender, represented respondent Billy Irl Glover at one of Glover's state trials on robbery charges, at which Glover was convicted. Petitioner Gary Babcock, the Oregon State Public Defender, represented Glover in Glover's unsuccessful state-court appeal from this and at least one other conviction. In an action brought under 42 U.S.C. 1983, Glover alleges that petitioners conspired with various state officials, including the trial and appellate court judges and the former Attorney General of Oregon, to secure Glover's conviction. Glover seeks neither reversal of his conviction nor compensatory damages, but asks instead for $5 million in punitive damages to be awarded against each petitioner. We conclude that public defenders are not immune from liability in actions brought by a criminal defendant against state public defenders who are alleged to have conspired with state officials to deprive the 1983 plaintiff of federal constitutional rights.", See Tower v. Glover, 467 U.S. 914 (1984).

Preliminary probable cause hearings are essential to justice as they require a court to evaluate the evidence and determine first whether a defendant is probably guilty or probably not guilty before the state continues to prosecute and deprive a person of Liberty. Probable cause hearings have always been a safeguard against unlawful arrests and unlawful prosecutions however the Federal Rules of Criminal procedure have recently changed, Rule 5.1 no longer requires a preliminary hearing is cases where the defendant has been indicted, which doesn't make sense since a prosecutor isn't required to present exculpatory evidence to the grand jury, See United States v. Williams, 504 U.S. 36 (1992). The previous version of rule 5.1 requires all prosecutions to hold a preliminary hearing unless waived by a defendant, See Mallory v. United States, 354 U.S. 449 (1957). The problem with the absence of a preliminary hearing is that it is designed to force defendants to sign plea agreements, See Peter Arenella, *Reforming the Federal Grand Jury and the State Preliminary Hearing to Prevent Conviction Without Adjudication*, 78 MICH. L. REV. 463 (1980). This does not protect the courts from unlawful arrests nor the rights of the accused, "This Prosecution should be stopped, not because some right of Casey's has been denied, but in order to protect the government. To protect it from illegal conduct of its officers. To preserve the purity of its courts.", See U.S. v. Russell, 411 U.S. 423 (1973)(Stewart, Brennan, Marshall). Arizona Rules of Criminal Procedure Rule 5.1(a) explicitly states that an adversary probable cause hearing is required under all circumstances: "A defendant has a right to a preliminary hearing if charged in a complaint with a felony. A preliminary hearing must commence before a magistrate no later than 10 days after the defendant's initial appearance if the defendant is in custody, or no later than 20 days after the defendant's initial appearance if the defendant is not in custody". Rule 5.1 (b) states: "The parties may waive a preliminary hearing but the waiver must be in writing and the defendant, defense counsel, and the State must sign it.". The police state of Arizona however has chose only to provide the bare minimum of due process as required by the U.S. Government, and contrary to the text of the Arizona Rules of Criminal Procedure. This is fraud. I received a letter from a state appointed attorney that stated a preliminary hearing was not required because of the indictment, following the Federal rules of criminal procedure. I had a similar experience in NYC where I was denied a preliminary hearing, although I was originally being charged with only a misdemeanor, and by the Federal Rules of Criminal Procedure, a probable cause hearing is still required. The state is however liable if they refuse to hear exculpatory evidence and keep a person detained or deprive them of liberty in any way, See Manuel v. City of Joliet, Ill., 580 S. Ct. 911 (2017). "Without (notice and a hearing), no citizen would be safe from the machinations of secret tribunals, and the most sane members of the community might be adjudged insane and landed in the madhouse.", See Ranking v. Howard, 633 F.2d 844 (9th Cir. 1980)(Fn.3); quoting In re Wellman, 3 Kan.App. 100, 45 P. 726, 727 (1896).

Law enforcement who make unlawful arrests may be sued and held liable in a court of law, whether the arrest was made in bad faith or not and even when the officer first attains warrant, See Malley v. Briggs, 475 U.S. 355 (1986). "A jury may be permitted to assess punitive damages in a § 1983 action when the defendant's conduct involves reckless or callous indifference to the plaintiff's federally protected rights, as well as when it is motivated by evil motive or intent", See Smith

v. Wade, 461 U.S. 30 (1983). An officer is also liable if he or she uses excessive force which is not "objectively reasonable", See Graham v. Connor, 490 U.S. 386 (1989). An officer is liable for excessive force even when a person is convicted or signs a plea agreement, See Smith v. City of Hemet, 394 F.3d 689 (9th Cir. 2005). Police are criminally liable for "excessive"and "unnecessary" force, See Koon v. U.S., 518 U.S. 81 (1996); Golden v. State, 1 S.C. 292 (1870); Skidmore v. State, 43 Tex. 93 (1875). An officer who makes an unlawful arrest can be criminally charged for kidnapping which is a capitol offense, See 18 U.S.C. §241 & §242. The U.S. Department of Justice website specifically describes The Act as being used against "police officers, prisons guards and other law enforcement officials, as well as judges, care providers in public health facilities, and others who are acting as public officials". The Government may be held liable for failing to enforce the law, See Cate v. Oldham, 707. F.2d 1176, 1185 (11th Cir. 1984). Public employees may be video recorded while on duty and sued for unlawful conduct, See Johnson v. Hawe, 388 F.3d 676 (9th Cir. 2004). Politicians have been maliciously prosecuted before upcoming elections, See Awabdy v. City of Adelanto, 368 F.3d 1062 (9th Cir. 2004); Donahoe v. Arpaio, 869 F. Supp.2d 1020 (2012). Retaliation for lawful exercise of one's rights presents a valid Federal claim, See Johnson v. Avery, 393 U.S. 483 (1969); Rizzo v. Dawson, 778 F.2d 527 (9th Cir. 1985); Dace v. Solem, 858 F.2d 385 (8th Cir. 1988); Cummings v. Harrison, 695 F.Supp.2d 1263 (2010). Employees of a private for profit corporation that are contracted by the state to run jails or prisons are not entitled to qualified immunity, See Richardson v. McKnight, 521 U.S. 399 (1997). "The tendency of those who execute the criminal laws of the country to obtain conviction by means of unlawful seizures... should find no sanction in the judgments of the courts, which are charged at all times with the support of the constitution", See Weeks v. United States, 232 U.S. 383 (1914). Police make false allegations, See Manuel v. City of Joliet, Ill., 580 S. Ct. 911 (2017). Here, officers alleged an unarmed man pulled an armed officer into his house and assaulted him while his armed partner watched, the defendant who's account of the incident radically differs from the two officer's version, later sued and won by jury trial after his charged were dismissed, See Borunda v. Richmond, 885 F.2d 1384 (9th Cir. 1988). False testimony from law enforcement has become increasingly common, See David N. Dorfman, *Proving the Lie: Litigating Police Credibility*, 26 Am. J. Crim. L. 455 (1999). The author discussed judges and police who work in a so called "grey area" of morality which is essentially another way of describing people too stupid to comprehend and value morality. Plaintiffs here, allege after being denied a fair trial in a criminal case, that police tampered with witnesses and knowingly presented false evidence and perjured testimony in court, See Venegas v. Wagner, 704 F.2d 1144 (9th Cir. 1983). Officials were found to have made false statements to the media and inspiring adverse media coverage after an unlawful arrest in Phoenix, See Gobel v. Maricopa County, 867 F.2d 1201 (9th Cir. 1989). A Victim of a false arrest prevailed on a malicious prosecution claim brought against the city of phoenix in state court , See Watzek v. Walker, 14 Ariz. App. 545 (1971).

Amendment VI of the United States Constitution states: "In all criminal prosecutions, the accused shall enjoy the right to a speedy and public trial". This is imperative in preventing prolonged civil rights violations of the presumed to be innocent and prejudice to the accused, See Barker v Wingo, 407 U.S. 514 (1972). In some cases often where the accused is guilty, delays can be part of the strategy. However, whether a person is released on bail or detained, delays tend to cause a deterioration of evidence. Likewise, sometime the government intentionally delays a case until it has to be dismissed, often because they didn't have a strong case to begin with. By delaying a case the government then extends its control over a person's life. "In sum, the body of New York State case law, like the decisions of other states, holds that dismissals for lack of timely prosecution should generally be considered, for purposes of a claim of malicious prosecution, a termination favorable to the accused.", See Murphy v. Lynn, 118 F.3d 938 (2nd Cir. 1997). Often the government is reluctant to immediately dismiss charges bringing attention to the fact that an arrest was illegal and the officers may be held liable. Confabulation is defined as memory error with fabrication and can be the result of unnecessary delays, this does not aid justice or adjudication. If a prosecution is found to have violated a defendants right to speedy trial the charges must be dismissed, "To rule otherwise would encourage state officials, hoping to shield wrongdoing officers and perhaps their municipalities from liability, to commence criminal prosecutions against the victims of that wrongdoing and simply hold the criminal charges in abeyance until a court is forced to dismiss the case after six or more months. Such a prolongation of proceedings can itself further injure a person maliciously accused without probable cause.", See Murphy v. Lynn, 118 F.3d 938 (2nd Cir. 1997). In 1974 Congress passed The Speedy Trial Act 18 U.S.C. 3161 which states, "the trial shall commence within seventy days". There are a number of exclusions however the standard for a typical prosecution is aimed between 30 and 70 days, See U.S. v. Loud hawk, 474 U.S. 302 (1986). This is applicable to the states, See U.S. v. Salerno, 481 U.S. 739 (1987); Lopez-Valenzuela v. Arpaio, 770 F.3d 772 (9th Cir. 2014). California's speedy trial is only sixty days, See California Penal Code - PEN § 1382. Arizona Rules of Criminal Procedure Rule 8.2 states a trial must commence, "No later than 150 days after arraignment if the defendant is in custody" and "No later than 180 days after arraignment if the defendant is released". Rule 8.6 states, "If the court determines, after excluding any applicable time periods, that a time limit established by these rules has been violated, the court must dismiss the prosecution with or without prejudice". The speedy trial clock starts at the time of arrest or public charge, See Doggett v. United States, 505 U.S. 647 (1992). The clock my not be stopped while a defendant is being charged, See Klopfer v. North Carolina, 386 U.S. 213 (1967). I was unconstitutionally detained in Arizona for over three years, 39 months to be exact, before my charges were dismissed. My trial in NY Commenced 16 months after the unlawful arrest. Both of these cases are examples of prosecutions in violation of Speedy Trial.

Bernhard Goetz shot and wounded four men in a NYC subway in 1984 and was regarded a hero. He was called a "The subway vigilante" by the Press. Despite tremendous public support he was criminally charged but acquitted on all counts except for illegally possessing a fire arm. Goetz volunteered to make a two hour video statement to police where he defended his actions as self-defense. He was a college graduate and had been mugged and beat up before. On the night of the shooting he was confronted by four young men who said "Give me five dollars". Goetz then pulled at his revolver and fired five shots. He showed absolutely no remorse for shooting the men. When asked about it he said when he saw the men's intentions for him, "My intention was to murder them, to hurt them, to make them suffer as much as possible." and "If I had more bullets, I would have shot 'em all again and again. My problem was I ran out of bullets.". This approach on the use of self-defense apparently worked well for Mr. Goetz.

On February 28th 1993 a firefight began between the Branch Davidians and federal law enforcement near Waco, Texas when the ATF attempted to execute a search and arrest warrant for their leader David Koresh. The siege lasted for fifty one days. Four federal agents were killed and twenty two more were injured. The

FBI took over shortly after the failed raid. The Mount Carmel Center Compound eventually was burnt down after authorities pumped flammable CS gas into the building. Seventy nine people died in the fire, twenty one of which were under the age of sixteen. This was one of the biggest events in U.S. History. Of the survivors, all eleven criminal defendants were acquitted by jury of conspiracy to murder federal officers. All eleven of the survivors made a successful self-defense assertion arguing the ATF shot first, See United States v. Branch, 91 F.3d 699 (5th Cir. 1996). Their successful self-defense claim was premised on the use of excessive force by federal agents. This is an example of what excessive force leads to. I do not believe the assertion that the Davidians set fire to the compound and then stayed inside and burnt to death. The U.S. Attorney general Janet Reno and all the supervising law enforcement officers should have been prosecuted for pumping flammable gas into the compound because that was excessive force. They could still be charged for ninety seven counts of involuntary manslaughter, See 18 U.S.C. 1112. There have been at least four documentaries made about this incident, See *Waco: Rules of Engagement* (1997); *Waco: Madman or Messiah* (2018); *Waco: A New Revelation* (2000); *Waco: The Big Lie* (1993). I think many of the allegations against David Koresh (the leader of he Branch Davidians) may have been exaggerated. There were claims that he was sleeping with underage girls. A six month investigation by the Texas Child Protection Services reported no evidence of child abuse. Either way the federal authorities would have no jurisdiction for such allegations. David Koresh had at least fifteen wives and at least one hundred people thought he was a prophet. There is a lot of video of him and the Branch Davidians that show they were usually very peaceful people. This incident proves there are sociopaths in the government. Think of the message it sends to not to prosecute for this use of excessive force. "It's not a crime to think you're Jesus" = Dick Reavis.

Qualified immunity is a major problem in this country. It shields government employees from civil liability. Today we have less protections from government than Europeans because they don't have qualified immunity and often have unarmed police. I think the concept of providing immunity for someone who has done something illegal is unconstitutional and was a shortfall of. Furthermore countries in Europe do not have qualified immunity. Killings by police is the U.S. are over 6,500% higher rate than in England and Whales. Police in the U.S. Have usually less than six months of training. In Europe training often lasts over three years. If we don't want police to act like gestapo law enforcement our policies need to change. Qualified immunity may be overruled by Congress or The Supreme Court of The United States. In an act of judicial policy-making the U.S. Supreme Court created the doctrine of clearly established law requirement, "We therefore hold that government officials performing discretionary functions, generally are shielded from liability for civil damages insofar as their conduct does not violate clearly established statutory or constitutional rights of which a reasonable person would have known." the court however then stated "If the law was clearly established, the immunity defense ordinarily should fail, since a reasonably competent public official should know the law governing his conduct.", See Harlow v. Fitzgerald, 457 U.S. 800 (1982). The problem is that many of the U.S. Circuit Courts and District Courts have taken it upon themselves to define clearly established law. They often rule that there is no case precedent and that particular acts even reckless and intentional do not qualify. However the notion that unconstitutional acts must also have case precedent describing very similar acts unconstitutional has been overruled, "the Court of Appeals required that the facts of previous cases be 'materially similar' to Hope's situation. This rigid gloss on the qualified immunity standard, though supported by Circuit precedent, is not consistent with our cases.", See Hope v. Pelzer, 536 U.S. 730 (2002); See also United States v. Lanier, 520 U.S. 259 (1997); Taylor v. Riojas, 592 U.S. ___ (2020).

According to the United Nations Handbook on Police Accountability, Oversight and Integrity an effective police accountability system should involves an independent oversight committee that enables civilian oversight of law enforcement conduct. This helps the public have confidence in their police and helps police maintain a moral authority. Many cities and states are adopting this reform. I strongly support this movement. They are often known as a civilian oversight agency or citizen review board. The citizen review board provides victims of police misconduct to voice their concerns and lodge a report. The NACOLE (National Association for Civilian Oversight of Law Enforcement) reported that of the sixty four oversight committees in the U.S. over half had no authority for independent investigations. These committees need power and resources to be effective. The committee should be able to investigate the allegations and make recommendations for disciplinary action and prosecution. The use of a fire arm or the killing of a suspect should automatically initiate committee review.

In Europe nineteen countries have unarmed police. The United states massively outnumbers most European countries in killings by police and law enforcement rarely face consequences for unlawful conduct. The prosecution and conviction for the murder of George Floyd was an exception. In 2020 there were 1,125 people killed by police in the U.S. Alone. There were four hundred and nine white people killed by police and two hundred forty seven black people killed by police in 2020. In many European countries the citizens don't have guns however in Iceland Citizens have guns and only one person has been killed by police in the history of the country. In the united states there are over 18,000 law enforcement agencies. This makes uniform training and discipline very difficult. In Europe many countries have a single police force. There are also nineteen countries have unarmed police. Officers don't need firearms to conduct traffic stops. I think it's time we rethink our militarization of police in the U.S. And consider disarming traffic police. We obviously don't want homicidal police driving around pulling people over. Police may retain firearms at a centralized location and dispatched only when needed.

On the morning of November 26, 1965 agents of the Federal Bureau of Narcotics entered the home of Webster Bivens and arrested him for alleged narcotics violations without probable cause. Justice Brennan delivered the opinion of the Court, "The agents manacled petitioner in front of his wife and children, and threatened to arrest the entire family. They searched the apartment from stem to stern. Thereafter, petitioner was taken to the federal courthouse in Brooklyn, where he was interrogated, booked, and subject to a visual strip search... Petitioner claimed to have suffered great humiliation, embarrassment, and mental suffering as a result of the agents' unlawful conduct, and sought $15,000 damages from each of them." The U.S. District court dismissed the complaint for lack of federal jurisdiction and failure to state a claim for which relief may be granted. The Court of appeals affirmed. The Supreme Court of The United States reversed, "Petitioner's complaint states a federal cause of action under the Fourth Amendment for which damages are recoverable upon proof of injuries resulting from the federal agents' violation of that Amendment." Justice Harlan wrote in concurring opinion, "For the reasons set forth below, I am of the opinion that federal courts do have the power to award damages for violation of 'constitutionally protected interests' and I agree with the Court that a traditional judicial remedy such as damages is appropriate to the vindication of the personal interests protected by the Fourth Amendment...

Thus the interest which Bivens claims = to be free from official conduct in contravention of the Fourth Amendment = is a federally protected interest... But I do not think that the fact that the interest is protected by the Constitution rather than statute or common law justifies the assertion that federal courts are powerless to grant damages in the absence of explicit congressional action authorizing the remedy.", See Bivens v. Six Unknown Named Agents of Federal Bureau of Narcotics, 403 U.S. 388 (1971).

The "Nuremberg defense" has two definitions: 1) "The supposed defense that one is not liable for acts done at the request of a superior; specific., a person's claim that he or she was 'just following orders' and therefore should not be held responsible for actions taken... The term comes from the Nuremberg war-crimes trials after World War II (1945-1946)" and 2) "The defense asserted by a member of the military who has been charged with the crime of failing to obey an order and who claims that the order was illegal, esp. that the order would result in a violation of international law.", See Black's Law Dictionary, West Publishing Co. (2016). It is important that all government employees are considered fully liable for any unlawful conduct whether or not by the orders of a superior and that they know it. It is important for every member of the police or military have plenty of incentives not to break the law in the first place.

In 1989 estimates of hundreds to thousands of college students were killed in the Tiananmen Square Massacre in Beijing, China when protests were forcibly suppressed with gun fire. On May 4th, 1970 U.S. National Guard fired on College student protesters at Kent State University, Ohio killing four and injuring nine more. "In these cases the personal representatives of the estates of three students who died in that episode seek damages against the Governor, the Adjutant General, and his assistant, various named and unnamed officers and enlisted members of the Ohio National Guard, and the president of Kent State University". The complaint was dismissed by the U.S. District Court and the U.S. Court of Appeals affirmed. The Supreme Court of The United States reversed and ruled, "We hold that dismissal was inappropriate at this stage of the litigation and accordingly reverse the judgments and remand for further proceedings", See Scheuer v. Rhodes, 416 U.S. 232 (1974).

CHAPTER 8

Here is a case where a man shoots a deputy trying to make an unlawful arrest with a twelve gauge in self-defense then is exonerated by the courts, See Jones v. State, 26 Tex. App. 1 (1888). Here, a victim of a threat fires his shotgun four times in rapid succession at an opponent shooting him dead and is then exonerated, See State v. Hendrix, 270 S.C. 653 (1978). And where it was ruled that as long as there is a reasonable doubt that a homicide was not committed in lawful self-defense, there is also a reasonable doubt of the guilt of the accused and where an officer was shot dead while trying to make an arrest for a misdemeanor without a warrant then exonerated, See Plummer v. State, 135 Ind. 308 (1893). "A man may repel force by force in the defence of his person, habitation, or property, against one or many who manifestly intend and endeavor, by violence or surprise, to commit a known felony on either. In such a case he is not obliged to retreat, but may pursue his adversary till he find himself out of danger; and if, in a conflict between them, he happen to kill, such killing is justifiable. The right of self-defence in cases of this kind is founded on the law of nature; and is not, nor can be, superseded by any law or society.", See Runyan v. State, 57 Ind. 80 (1877); quoting Wharton on Criminal Law, Vol. 2, § 1019. See where two witnesses testify they saw a defendant strike the deceased first, prior to making a fatal wound with a knife and then a new trial was ordered for prejudicial error because of one comment made by the judge, See State v. Blue, 356 N.C. 79 (2002). And where it was ruled a person had the right to stand his ground after killing an unarmed attacker, See Miller v. State, 74 Ind.1 (1881). See where it was ruled that any citizen has the right to resist any attempt to put any illegal restraint upon his liberty, See Noles v. State, 26 Ala. 31 (1855). See where it was ruled a person has the right to lawfully use deadly force against an officer attempting to effectuate an arrest with an invalid warrant, See Agee v. State, 64 Ind. 340 (1878). Preemptive force is when a person responds to a threat before an assault is made upon him or her. This right is supported by State and Federal law but the threat must be immediate, See Badelk v. United States, 177 U.S. 529 (1900); See also Jones v. State, 26 Tex. App. 1 (1888). "No man can set his foot upon my ground without my license, but he is liable to an action, though the damage be nothing, which is proved by every declaration in trespass where the defendant is called upon to answer for bruising the grass and even treading upon the soil. If he admits the fact, he is bound to show, by way of justification, that some positive law has justified or excused him. The justification is submitted to the judges, who are to look into the books, and see if such a justification can be maintained by the text of the statute law, or by the principles of the common law.", See Boyd v United States, 116 U.S. 616 (1886).

The Retreat Doctrine states that when the initial aggressor of an altercation retreats his self-defense rights resuscitate. In the NYC case I had clearly retreated from the altercation with the bell hop and attempted to select my floor inside the elevator to go to my apartment. Even if he was unaware (which he wasn't) of his fault for physically trying to stop me in the first place, he certainly had no right to further attack me when he had seen my retreat. "If a person, under the provocation of offensive language, assaults the speaker personally, but in such a way as to show that there is no intention to do him serious bodily harm, and then retires under such circumstances as show that he does not intend to do anything more, but in good faith withdraws from further contest, his right of self-defense is restored... the court, after adverting to the general rule that the aggressor cannot be heard to urge in his justification a necessity for the killing which was produced by his own wrongful act, said: This rule, however, is not absolute and universal application. An exception to it exists in cases where, although the defendant originally provoked the conflict, he withdraws from it in good faith, and clearly announces his desire for peace. If he be pursued after this, his right of self-defense, though once lost, revives", See Rowe v. U.S., 164 U.S. 546 (1896).

In 1968 the United States Supreme Court made one of the worst rulings they've ever made when they made it lawful to stop suspects on less than probably cause. The Supreme Court dismantled the barrier between police and citizens. The court stated, "nothing we say today is to be taken as indicating approval of police conduct outside the legitimate investigative sphere", as if they predicted problems with their ruling. The ruling gave police the authority to make stops on "reasonable suspicion", which expanded the authority of law enforcement tremendously. Judge Douglas made a epic dissent arguing if probable cause was the requirement for a magistrate to issue a warrant then police should have no greater authority. He also stated, "To give the police greater power than a magistrate is to take a long step down the totalitarian path.", See Terry v. Ohio, 392 U.S. 1 (1968) (Douglas). I support the overruling of this case. The Supreme Court of The United States has overruled over 300 of it's own cases.

On December 20th 1980 Rhode Island State Police conducted a court-authorized wiretap of a phone call. "After reviewing the logsheet for December 20, petitioner decided that the call from 'Dr. Shogun' was incriminating, because in drug parlance 'toking' means smoking marihuana and 'rolling her thing' refers to rolling a marihuana cigarette... Local and statewide newspapers published the fact that respondents, who are prominent members of their community, had been arrested and charged with drug possession. The charges against respondents were subsequently dropped when the grand jury to which the case was presented did not return and indictment... Respondents brought an action under 42 U.S.C. 1983 in the United States District Court for the District of Rhode Island charging, inter alia, that petitioner, in applying for warrants for their arrest, violated their rights under the Fourth and Fourteenth Amendments. The case was tried to a jury, and at the close of respondents' evidence, petitioner moved for and was granted a directed verdict. The District Court's primary justification for directing a verdict was that the act of the judge in issuing the arrest warrants for respondents broke the causal chain between petitioner's filing of a complaint and respondents' arrest... The United States Court of Appeals for the First Circuit reversed". The Supreme Court of The United States ruled qualified immunity "provides ample protection to all but the plainly incompetent or those who knowingly violate the law" and that "The analogous question in this case is whether a reasonably well-trained officer in petitioner's position would have known that his affidavit failed to establish probable cause and that he should not have applied for the warrant. If such was the case, the officer's application for a warrant was not objectively reasonable, because it created the unnecessary danger of an unlawful arrest... The judgment of the Court of Appeals is affirmed, and the case is remanded for further proceedings consistent with this opinion... Respondents each sought $1 million in compensatory damages and $1 million in punitive damages", See Malley v. Briggs, 475 U.S. 355 (1986).

Illinois' Governor Otto J. Kerner and prison officials were sued by an inmate named Francis Haines who claimed for $500,000 after he was deprived of Liberty without a Hearing. "Petitioner's pro se complaint was premised on alleged action of prison officials placing him in solitary confinement as a disciplinary measure after he had struck another inmate on the head with a shovel following a verbal altercation. The assault by petitioner on another inmate is not denied. Petitioner's pro se complaint included general allegation of physical injuries suffered while in disciplinary confinement and denial of due process in the steps leading to that confinement... The District Court granted respondents motion under Rule 12 (b) (6) of the Federal Rules of Civil Procedure to dismiss the complaint for failure to state a claim upon which relief could be granted... The Court of Appeals affirmed... The only issue now before us is petitioner's contention that the District Court erred in dismissing his pro se complaint without allowing him to present evidence on his claims... We cannot say with assurance that under the allegations of the pro se complaint, which we hold to less stringent standards than formal pleadings drafted by lawyers, it appears 'beyond doubt that the plaintiff can prove no set of facts in support of his claim which would entitle him to relief.' Conley v. Gibson, 355 U.S. 41, 45 -46 (1957)", See Haines v. Kerner, 404 U.S. 519 (1972); 427 F.2d 71 (7th Cir. 1970).

I have no lawful priors only a series of false arrests by illegitimate police after the arrest in NY as you can see by the date of a subsequent arrest. I was almost twenty seven before I ever spent time in jail. The police reports from NY in 2011 show I had no criminal history or pending warrants at the time the false arrest, See Taebel v. Sonberg 2:18 CV 00046-GMS, filed in the phoenix U.S. District Court, or

Taebel v. Sonberg 2:18 CV 00138-TLN (PS) filed in the U.S. District Court of Sacramento. Taebel v. Brown et al 1:18 CV 00192-TWP-MJD shows a false arrests in California due to prejudice from the conviction in NY. I had no criminal record however just weeks after the jury's verdict I was unlawfully arrested again within in a matter of weeks. After a traffic stop in on Hollywood Blvd. Just west of N. Highland Ave I was arrested for an alleged DUI however I was sober. The officer never even asked me to take a field sobriety test. He had no evidence I was DUI or any reason to arrest me. They were apparently in the business of making arrests then attempting to justify them afterwards which is has been ruled unconstitutional by the U.S. Supreme Court a number of times, See Johnson v. United States, 333 U.S. 10 (1948); Henry v. United States, 361 U.S. 98 (1959); Dunaway v. New York, 442 U.S. 200 (1979). He asked me to step out of the vehicle and allow him to Terry Frisk me then proceeded to unlawfully arrest me after seeing I had nothing illegal on me. The officer got violent and wrestled me to the ground after asking me to drop my phone video recording and I refused. At the police station a big officer asked me to take a "dark room test" and I was afraid they wanted to rape me like Abner Louima before I even knew about Abner Louima so I just said "No" then refused to speak. I was in handcuffs. They wanted to drug test me at the police station but even police officers know the test results can be faked, See Gonzalez v. Bratton, 147 F. Supp. 2d 180 (S.D.N.Y. 2001). I had already been arrested and I didn't think it mattered. They likely would have just made up another reason to attempt to justify the arrest in the police reports. They need probably cause at the time of arrest or the law requires the charges to be dismissed. If I agreed to take a blood test and they faked the results it would have been used against me. I took a lab drug test at a clinic after release and passed for all substances. I had taken video of the arrest from my iPhone with an app that immediately backed up video online similar to the ACLU app. These apps are designed to report unlawful police conduct and the video is automatically saved on a remote drive in case an officer breaks or steals the phone. The DMV reviewed the video and drug test results and dismissed the allegations preventing my license from being suspended but a criminal charge of DUI refusal remained in court. The officer attempted to press charges for resisting arrest however that was declined by the District Attorney's Office after they reviewed the video. After NY I had lost all faith in the criminal justice system and in trial by jury. The need to be able to dismiss charges after an unjustified arrest through a probable cause hearing without relying on a jury trial became very apparent. I had personally seen a jury get it wrong against massive amounts of exonerating evidence. I spoke to a lawyer over the phone who was very helpful. He said the lawfulness of the arrest can be challenged in a probable cause hearing. He also said if the judge denies the motion to dismiss for lack of probable cause the decision may be appealed. I met with several lawyers and showed each of the video. They all said the arrest was illegal. One said he recommended to take it to trial and he would file a Civil suit after the dismissal. As much as I liked to hear we could sue I didn't trust a jury trial which I considered playing Russian Roulette. I retained Daniel Perlman because he thought he could get the charges thrown out without going to trial. Then he came back and with a plea deal for the "lowest class of misdemeanor" almost an infraction. I didn't want to go to trial so I signed a plea agreement because I was coerced by a corrupt criminal justice system. The officer put an illegal 30 day hold on the vehicle and the lawyer was able to immediately get my vehicle back. This unconstitutional misdemeanor conviction should be able to be overturned. This established a record of unjustified arrests. If a person unjustly arrested twice it is likely a third arrest would be unjustified. That's just math.

"Whoever, under color of any law, statute, ordinance, regulation, or custom, willfully subjects any person in any State, Territory, Commonwealth, Possession, or District to the deprivation of any rights, privileges, or immunities secured or protected by the Constitution or laws of the United States, ... shall be fined under this title or imprisoned not more than one year, or both; and if bodily injury results from the acts committed in violation of this section or if such acts include the use, attempted use, or threatened use of a dangerous weapon, explosives, or fire, shall be fined under this title or imprisoned not more than ten years, or both; and if death results from the acts committed in violation of this section or if such acts include kidnapping or an attempt to kidnap, aggravated sexual abuse, or an attempt to commit aggravated sexual abuse, or an attempt to kill, shall be fined under this title, or imprisoned for any term of years or for life, or both, or may be sentenced to death.", See 18 U.S.C. §242. In Arizona I was "kidnapped" and assaulted with "dangerous weapons" by use of spike strips and a PIT by police who willfully violated my right to flee from an arrest without the threat of deadly force, See Tennessee v. Garner, 471 U.S. 1 (1985); Orn v. City of Tacoma, 949 F.3d 1167 (9th Cir. 2020). This was a ten year offense committed by the police in Arizona on television in addition to kidnapping which is a capitol offense, See 18 U.S.C. §241 & §242. Here, police were prosecuted for the assault of Rodney King under the Civil Rights Act, See Koon v. U.S., 518 U.S. 81 (1996). "Every person who under color of state law subjects or causes to be subjected, any citizen of the United States or other person within the jurisdiction thereof to the deprivation of any rights, privileges, or immunities and laws, shall be liable to the person injured in an action at law....", See 42 U.S.C. §1983; See also 28 U.S.C. §1343. The civil rights Act is comprised of 18 U.S.C. §241 & §242 and 42 U.S.C. §1983.

Judicial immunity is a serious problem in this country however judges who act in "clear absence of all jurisdiction" of state and federal law may be sued, See Stump v. Sparkman, 435 U.S. 349 (1978); Forrester v. White, 484 U.S. 219 (1988). Police and other government employees often hide behind judges with judicial immunity who make significant constitutional violations and don't expect any repercussions. The Problem with judicial immunity is it takes the power of law enforcement out of the hands of the citizen and into the hands of lawless prosecutions as does prosecutorial immunity. Prosecutors may be sued however for knowingly presenting false evidence, See Kalina v. Fletcher, 522 U.S. 118 (1997). There is little down side to allowing a jury to hear a case and for them to determine whether government's conduct was or was not reasonable. Judges may be criminally liable before they are Civilly liable under the Civil Rights Act "Judges who would willfully discriminate on the ground of race or otherwise would willfully deprive the citizen of his constitutional rights, as this complaint alleges, must take account of 18 U.S.C. 242", See O'Shea v. Littleton, 414 U.S. 488 (1974). "A state judge can be found criminally liable under 242 although that judge may be immune from damages under 1983", See Dennis v. Sparks, 449 U.S. 24(1980) (Fn.5); United States v. Lanier, 520 U.S. 259 (1997); United States v. Classic, 313 U.S. 299 (1941). Judges act unlawfully and aren't required to have any legal training or college degree, See Gregory v. Thompson, 500 F.2d 59, 63 (9th Cir. 1974). A judge who agrees to rule in a party's favor prior to a hearing or trial, is in clear and complete absence of jurisdiction and is liable, See Ranking v. Howard, 633 F.2d 844 (9th Cir. 1980). Judges may be liable for defamation motivated by racial prejudice, See Harris v. Harvey 605 F.2d 330 (7th Cir. 1979). And of course a judge may be liable for acting as a prosecutor, judge and jury, See Lopez v. Vanderwater, 620 F.2d 1229 (7th Cir. 1980). The judges in NYC and in Phoenix should be prosecuted for their violations of the constitution and accessory to kidnapping under the Civil Rights Act. Judicial immunity stems from the English monarchy and has no place in a modern democracy.

The Fundamental implication of The 2nd Amendment is the absolute right of Self-Defense, See McDonald v. Chicago, 561 U.S. 742 (2010). The victim of an attack has the right to objectively debilitate an opponent, See Brown v. US, 256 U.S. 335 (1921) where a defendant prevailed in court after shooting the attacker multiple times and after he was already down. A Man certainly has no duty to retreat when going about his business or on the property of his dwelling. Self-defense is a crime deterrent and natural justice. Self-defense and right to "stand your ground" is about a man's right to be a man and not be harassed by parasites. Beware, it's been my experience that courts don't always follow the Supreme Court's wisdom on self-defense, See Brown v. U.S., 256 U.S. 335 (1921); Rowe v. United States, 164 U.S. 546 (1896); Badelk v. United States, 177 U.S. 529 (1900). They need a lesson on self-defense and the laws of man. Anyone who reads those three cases likely knows more about self-defense than nine of ten lawyers or judges. In a case where a defendant was found guilty of manslaughter after shooting an assailant with whom he had started a feud by kicking him on the leg while at his table in the lobby of a hotel the U.S. District court judge stated, "Neither one of them was required to retreat under such circumstances, because the hotel or temporary stopping place of a man may be regarded as his dwelling place, and the law of retreat in a case like that is different from what it would be on the outside.", The U.S. Supreme court reversed the conviction, See Rowe v. United States, 164 U.S. 546 (1896). Most state statutes do not require an attacker to use unlawful force, they only require a person to have a reasonable apprehension of unlawful physical force, See Ny Penal Law § 35.15; AZ ST § 13-404; CALCRIM 3470; or Florida Statute § 776.012. By the NY statute and further research I've done on the subject, I would have to say that there was nothing illegal in the allegations in NYC. Even though they fictitiously claimed he was punched four times and without first using unlawful force it was obvious that a reasonable person could have anticipated the use of unlawful force by the Bellhop given his aggression that was also captured on video. Even if his false testimony was true they still couldn't prove beyond a reasonable doubt that it wasn't self-defense. Even the European courts recognize the right of "preemptive force", See Jonathan Herring, *Criminal Law* §15.4.2, London, Palgrave Law Masters, Published 2017. "The strongest reason for the people to retain the right to keep and bear arms, as a last resort, to protect themselves against tyranny in government."= Thomas Jefferson. See how the courts have ruled on self-defense cases since the beginning of our country. Watch the Media case: State of Florida v. George Zimmerman (2013). "Many respectable writers agree if a man reasonably believes that he is in immediate danger of death or grievous bodily harm from his assailant he may stand his ground and that if he kills him he has not succeeded the bounds of lawful-self defence. That has been the decision of this court.", See Brown v. U.S., 256 U.S. 335 (1921). To appose the right of a man to stand his ground would encourage the the parasites and criminals. Self-Defense puts justice in the hands of every man. It is a form of citizen law enforcement similar to civil litigation. The liberals threaten the right of self-defense because they apparently don't understand it. The principals of self-defense are apparently too complicated for many of the liberals similar to the principles of the Constitutional law. Our country was founded by those who valued their freedom.

In a 6-3 decision written by Justice Clark The Supreme Court of the united states established the fruit-of-the-poisonous-tree doctrine. "Appellant stands convicted of knowingly having had in her possession and under her control certain lewd and lascivious books, pictures, and photographs in violation of §2905.34 of

Ohio's Revised Code... At the trial no search warrant was produced by the prosecution, nor was the failure to produce one explained or accounted for... We hold that all evidence obtained by searches and seizures in violation of the Constitution is, by that same authority, inadmissible in a state court... the purpose of the exclusionary rule is to deter = to compel respect for the constitutional guaranty in the only effectively available way = by removing the incentive to disregard it... Thus the State, by admitting evidence unlawfully seized, serves to encourage disobedience to the Federal Constitution which it is bound to uphold... Nothing can destroy a government more quickly than its failure to observe its own laws, or worse, its disregard of the charter of its own existence... If the government becomes a lawbreaker, it breeds contempt for law, it invites every man to become a law unto himself, it invites anarchy", See Mapp v. Ohio, 367 U.S. 643 (1961).

Officers can be held liable for an illegal search, See Monroe v. Pape, 365 U.S. 167 (1961); Larez v. City of Los Angeles, 946 F.2d 630 (9th Cir. 1991). Anyone who has been the victim of a false arrest, has the right to file a claim without delay, the suit should not be barred while charges are pending unless the state has already reached a conviction, See Heck v. Humphrey, 512 U.S. 477 (1994). A plaintiff may be better off taking immediate civil action against a false arrest regardless of pending charges in criminal court, See Wallace v. kato, 549 U.S. 1362 (2007). In cases where a state fails to respect a persons United States constitutional rights, "civil actions or criminal prosecutions, commenced in a State court may be removed by the defendant to the district court", See 28 U.S.C. §1443. A Defendant to a malicious prosecution can sue for injunctive relief, declaratory decree or monetary accruing damages in Federal Court. The United States courts however have what's called an abstention doctrine which states only plaintiffs who can make a showing of bad faith, harassment or other unusual circumstances are entitled to relief against a malicious prosecution, See Younger v. Harris, 401 U.S. 37 (1971); Mitchum v. Foster, 407 U.S. 255 (1972); Carey v. Piphus, 435 U.S. 247 (1978); See Also Dombrowski v. Pfister, 380 U.S. 479 (1965). This rule derived from previous rulings which adhered to the traditional prerequisite of a showing of imminent irreparable injury. "It is well settled that the loss of First Amendment freedoms for even minimal periods of time constitutes irreparable injury justifying the grant of a preliminary injunction.", See Cate v. Oldham, 707 F.2d 1176 (11th Cir. 1983); quoting Deerfield Medical Center v. City of Deerfield Beach, 661 F.2d 328, 338 (5th Cir. Unit B 1981). "The first inquiry in any §1983 suit, therefore, is whether the plaintiff has been deprived of a right 'secured by the constitution and laws'.", See Baker v. McCollan, 443 U.S. 137 (1979). "But one general limitation the court has repeatedly recognized is that the concept of collateral estoppel cannot apply when the party against whom the earlier decision is asserted did not have a 'full and fair opportunity' to litigate that issue in the earlier case", See Allen v. McCurry, 449 U.S. 90 (1980). Intentionally unlawful, malicious or oppressive conduct warrants punitive damages, See Smith v. Wade, 461 U.S. 30 (1983); Dang V. Cross, 422 F.3d 800 (2005); Giron v. City of Alexander, 693 F.Supp2d 904 (2010); see also Braillard v. Maricopa County, 224 Ariz. 481 (2010). Police have been known to overreact and use excessive force, See Orn v. City of Tacoma, 949 F.3d 1167 (9th Cir. 2020); Cable v City of Phoenix, 647 F. App'x 780 (9th Cir. 2016); Young v City of Los Angeles 655 F.3d 1156, 1163 (9th Cir. 2011) ; Binkovich v. Barthelemy, 672 Fed. Appx. 648 (9th Cir. 2016). Vague statutes hampering the 1st amendment right to peaceably assemble are invalid, See Coates v. City of Cincinnati, 404 U.S. 611 (1971). Freedom of speech has minimal limitations, See Cohen v. California, 403 U.S. 15 (1971). A man has a 1st Amendment right verbally challenge an officer to fight, See City of Houston, Tex. v. Hill, 482 U.S. 451 (1987). Even

Legislators can be sued for defamatory statements made to the media, See Hutchinson v. Proxmire, 443 U.S. 111 (1979). When determining whether government employees are entitled to immunity, the court accepts the allegations of a complaint as true and prosecutors have no immunity for false statements made in affidavit, See Kalina v. Fletcher, 522 U.S. 118 (1997). Law is philosophy and philosophy is everything. The study of law is for those who are passionate about principles and the physics of life. It is the study of the way things are and the way it should be. It is always common sense applied to sometimes complicated situations. It is the fine study of pragmatic sense and I like pragmatic sense. I began reading law in New York after my unlawful arrest and found the law to be exonerating in many ways. The law has always made sense to me and works in my favor.

The importance of Philosophy and fundamental theory became important to me early in life. I remember my girlfriend in high school telling me I would change the World. Philosophy for me began on that basis. Assuming I would inevitably change the World, however big or small, I then asked myself what kind of effect did I want to have and how did I plan to achieve that outcome. In order for it to make sense for other people to respect you, you must believe in having a positive effect on the people around you. Morality scientifically makes sense. As it makes sense to think optimistically and positively. It is a primitive human condition to be amoral. There are tremendous health effects which stem from philosophy. Positive or negative, just as there tremendous benefits from exercise. I think like a doctor who is conscientious and believes in living a healthy life. With that comes positivism. Even for those who don't believe in Karma, it's hard to deny that good things usually come to good people. Morality is simply having consideration for yourself and others. The smarter a person is, the easier it is for them to have more consideration but everyone must try. To understand morality is to understand the bigger picture which not everyone can do. It's a moral obligation that the people who understand Ethics inform the ignorant. Which is one reason successful people are usually personable. Most of my friends would say I am the last person they would have thought to ever get arrested. Probably because I threaten to call the police for littering. And because I honestly despise criminal behavior and genuinely think that it stems from a shallow and erred philosophy. Many criminals are deranged homosexuals. When it comes to morality the priority is law and keeping people from breaking it. Something the world could do a much better job at. Lawful behavior that may be considered unethical is a secondary concern. For example I don't usually curse or sleep with married women. Unless their spouse don't mind. I always tell women to be good to their husbands. Some people consider the possibility that life on earth is heaven and they might consider themselves agnostic. On Semester At Sea we discussed "Pascal's Wager" where he argues that it is very little trouble to be a good person and for even those who doubt the existence of Heaven and Hell, living an immoral life is not worth the risk. I always idolized the greatest philosophers on earth Socrates, Aristotle, Plato, Pascal, Martin Luther King, Jr., the framers of the country and Don Juan. To best understand law, it is ideal to study both Law around the World and the History of Law in this Country.

The role of The U.S. Attorney General originated in the Judiciary Act of 1789 with an annual salary of $1,500. His part time duties were, " to prosecute and conduct all suits in the Supreme Court in which the United States shall be concerned, and to give his advice and opinion upon questions of law when required by the President of the United States, or when requested by the heads of any of the departments, touching any matters that may concern their departments", See First Congress Ch. XX Sec. 35. The U.S. Department of Justice was formed in 1870 under Ulysses S. Grant. The United States Attorney General was originally in the Judicial branch of government however when Washington D.C. became a state in 1889 the state constitution codified the role of the U.S. Attorney General in the Executive Branch. Today the U.S. Attorney general oversees an excess of 100,000 employees. According to U.S. Attorney General Merrick Garland, a primary purpose of The U.S. Department of Justice is to enforce the Civil Rights Act that I cited on TV.

CHAPTER 9

This chapter covers the History of The Supreme Court of the United States. The Federalist papers were published by Alexander Hamilton, John Jay and James Madison from 1787-1788. The Constitution was declared in effect after the War March 4th 1789. The First Acts of Congress were also passed in 1789. The Bill of Rights was passed in 1791. The next Amendments were ratified sporadically between 1798-1992. John Jay was appointed to The Supreme Court as Chief Justice in 1789.The U.S. Supreme Court ruled a state may be sued by an individual citizen of another state and default judgment may be entered without appearance, See Chisolm v. Georgia, 2 U.S. 419 (1793). John Marshall was appointed as Chief Judge of The United States Supreme Court in 1801. The Constitution is superior to any ordinary legislative act and The Supreme Court has the authority to overrule an act repugnant to The Constitution, See Marbury v. Madison, 5 U.S. 137 (1803). The first ruling that a state law was unconstitutional was for violating the contract clause, See Fletcher v. Peck, 10 U.S. 87 (1810). The U.S. Supreme Court has the authority of appellate review for all cases in which it does not have original jurisdiction, including review of state court's final decisions, See Martin v. Hunter's Lessee, 14 U.S. 304 (1816).The charter of a private corporation is a contract protected by the constitution from legislative interference, the New Hampshire law was ruled invalid, See Trustees of Dartmouth College v. Woodward, 17 U.S. 518 (1819). Chief Justice Marshall ruled in majority opinion that any state law that conflicts with a congressional act regulating commerce is void, See Gibbons v. Ogden, 22 U.S. 1 (1824). The Supreme Court upheld the delegation of power to the Federal courts using the necessary and proper clause, allowing congress to convey power to the lower Federal Courts, See Wayman v. Southard, 23 U.S. 1 (1825). Roger B. Taney was appointed as Supreme Court of The United States Chief Jude in 1836. In contracts between a state and private parties, any ambiguity must be interpreted in favor of the private parties, See Proprietors of the Charles River Bridge v. Proprietors of the Warren Bridge, 36 U.S. 420 (1837). Chief Judge Taney states the courts opinion that the authors of The Declaration of Independence and The U.S. Constitution did not feel that slaves were fit to associate with the white race, that all of the thirteen original colonies recognized slavery, See Dred Scott v. Sanford, 60 U.S. 393 (1856). Salmon P. Chase was appointed in 1864 as Chief Justice. Only those privileges and immunities of U.S. Citizens are protected by the Fourteenth Amendment and apply to citizens of another state, See The slaughterhouse cases, 83 U.S. 36 (1872). Morrison R. Waite was appointed as Chief Justice. The U.S. Supreme Court shot down and overruled a states claim that they had a right to police power, See Yick Wo v. Hopkins, 118 U.S. 356 (1886). Melville W. Fuller was appointed as Chief Justice in 1888. The Court ruled in majority opinion that state law requiring trains to provide separate facilities and cars for white and black passengers did not infringe upon the thirteenth or Fourteenth Amendments of The U.S. Constitution establishing the "separate but equal" doctrine, See Plessy v. Ferguson, 163 U.S. 537 (1896). The court upheld a ruling that a merger created a monopoly and was in violation of the 1890 Sherman Act, See Northern Securities

Co. v. United States, 193 U.S. 197 (1904). The Court ruled compulsory vaccine was not always unconstitutional, See Jacobson v. Commonwealth of Massachusetts, 197 U.S. 11 (1905). The U.S. Supreme Court ruled that a NY state law limiting exclusively Bakery workers to ten hours a day was a violation of equal protections, See Lochner v. New York, 198 U.S. 45 (1905). The Court ruled the Sherman Act against monopolies could regulate stockyards because they were acting in the stream of interstate commerce, See Swift & Company v. United States, 196 U.S. 375 (1905). Edawrd D. White was appointed as Chief Justice in 1910. The U.S. Supreme ruled on the espionage Act of 1917 and stating that freedom of speech and the press may be restrained if "The words used... create a clear and present danger", See Schenck v. United States, 249 U.S. 47 (1919). The migratory bird treaty Act was upheld, See Missouri v. Holland, 252 U.S. 416 (1920). William H. Taft was appointed as Chief Justice in 1921. It was ruled a citizen has no grounds to sue for the government's expenses arguably being misused tax money, See Frothingham v. Mellon, 262 U.S. 447 (1923). Nebraska passed a statute prohibiting all public and private schools from teaching any language other than English which was overruled by The U.S. Supreme Court, See Meyer v. Nebraska, 262 U.S. 390 (1923). The Supreme Court of The United States ruled the 1st Amendment and all of The Bill of Rights were applicable to the states, See Gitlow v. New York, 268 U.S. 652 (1925). The Supreme Court ruled the state may require children to attend school however the parents have the right to choose between private or public schools, See Pierce v. Society of sisters, 268 U.S. 510 (1925). It was ruled congress had the implied right to order compulsory witness testimony for investigative purposes as part of their legislative duty, See McGrain v. Daugherty, 273 U.S. 135 (1927). The U.S. Supreme Court upheld a conviction under the California Criminal Syndicate law for joining as a member of a socialist communist group advocating subversive action,

See Whitney v. California, 274 U.S. 357 (1927). Charles E. Hughes was appointed as Chief Justice in 1930. The Supreme Court ruled the right to effective assistance of counsel applies to the states, See Powell v. Alabama, 287 U.S. 45 (1932). The court ruled that in time of economic emergency government may pass law to alter pre-existing contracts to protect its citizens, See Home Building & Loan Association v. Blaisdell, 290 U.S. 398 (1934). The court upheld a state law passed in the wake of the great depression, that was a significant intrusion of the free economy, aimed to control milk prices, See Nebbia v. New York, 291 U.S. 502 (1934). The U.S. Supreme Court overruled the National Industrial Recovery Act of 1933, See Schechter Poultry Corp. v. United States, 295 U.S. 495 (1935). The Supreme Court overruled another congressional act, the Bituminous Coal Conservation Act (1935), See Carter v. Carter Coal Co., 298 U.S. 238 (1936). The Court ruled legislators do not have the power to regulate for public welfare, they only have the power to provide for the public welfare and to lay and collect taxes, See U.S. v. Butler, 297 U.S. 1 (1936). The Supreme Court upheld poll taxes of $1 to vote in Georgia, stating it was not an equal protections violation, which was not overruled until twenty nine years later, See Breedlove v. Suttles, Tax Collector, 302 U.S. 277 (1937). State and Federal Law apply in a Federal District court in suits of liability, See Erie Railroad Company v. Tompkins, 304 U.S. 64 (1938). The Supreme Court upheld an act which prohibited interstate commerce of filled milk for the interest of public welfare, See U.S. v. Carolene Products Co., 304 U.S. 144 (1938). A state statute in Oklahoma which denied African Americans the right to vote was ruled unconstitutional, See Lane v. Wilson, 307 U.S. 268 (1939). The U.S. Supreme Court ruled that city ordinances may not prohibit the distribution of information leaflets, See Schneider v. Irvington, 308 U.S. 147 (1939). William O. Douglas was appointed to the U.S. Supreme Court in 1939. The Supreme Court overruled an Alabama statute as a violation of The 1st

Amendments guarantee to free speech, freedom of the press and to peaceably assemble, See Thornhill v. Alabama, 310 U.S. 88 (1940). Justice Harlan F. Stone was appointed as chief Judge of The Supreme Court of The United States in 1941. The Supreme Court ruled that a California law that made it illegal to bring indigent folk into the state was unconstitutional, See Edwards v. California, 314 U.S. 160 (1941). The Court ruled that a statute which prohibited lewd, obscene, profane, libelous or insulting words which were intended to inflict injury or incite immediate breach of peace, was not unconstitutional, See Chaplinsky v. New Hampshire, 315 U.S. 568 (1942). A statute which required the sterilization of repeat criminal offenders was ruled a violation of The Fourteenth Amendment, See Skinner v. State of Oklahoma ex. Rel. Williamson, Attorney General, 316 U.S. 535 (1942). The U.S. Supreme Court upheld curfews on minorities perceived to be a potential threat during wartime, See Hirabayashi v. United States, 320 U.S. 81 (1943). The Supreme Court of The United States upheld orders from President Franklin Delano Roosevelt ordering all persons of foreign decent from countries with whom the U.S. Was at war with to be held in internment camps, See Korematsu v. United States, 323 U.S. 214 (1944). The Supreme Court ruled that "intent" for every element of a crime charged must be proven, See Screws v. United States, 325 U.S. 91 (1945). The Supreme Court overruled a state law limiting the number of train cars allowed to be in use, See Southern Pacific Co. v. Arizona, 325 U.S. 761 (1945). The Court held that reapportion of state legislative districts non justiciable. See Colegrove v. Green, 328 U.S. 549 (1946). The Court overruled a series of cases which required a naturalization oath for those seeking citizenship in which they would take up arms to defend the country in a time of war, the ruling provided they may serve in allegiance in military or other services without bearing arms if they show by clear and convincing evidence that it is for religious reasons, See Girouard v. United

States, 328 U.S. 61 (1946). Fred M. Vinson was appointed as Chief Judge. The Supreme Court declined to rule on the constitutionality of The Hatch Act of 1940 which prohibits federal employees of the executive branch from participating in lobby groups or political campaigns, See United Public Workers v. Mitchell, 330 U.S. 75 (1947). The Supreme Court ruled that a city ordinance which banned the use of sound amplification for matters of public concern, news and athletic events was unconstitutional, See Saia v. New York, 334 U.S. 558 (1948). The state cannot recognize or honor a covenant that stated "no part of this property shall be occupied by any person not of the Caucasian race" as it would be a violation of The Fourteenth Amendment to recognize the stipulation in a private agreement, See Shelley v. Kramer, 334 U.S. 1 (1948). The Supreme Court ruled "the forefathers, after consulting the lessons of history, designed our constitution to place obstacles in the way of a too permeating police surveillance, which they seem to think was a greater danger to a free people than the escape of some criminals from punishment", See United States v. Di Re, 332 U.S. 581 (1948). The Court ruled that contracts may not obligate parties to employ exclusively union or non union employees, See Lincoln Federal Labor Union v. Northwestern Iron & Metal Co., 355 U.S. 525 (1949). The United States Supreme Court overruled a city regulation which limits the First Amendments Freedom of Speech Clause, See Terminiello v. City of Chicago, 337 U.S. 1 (1949). The Court upheld the Smith Act stating that "intent" to advocate government overthrow by force and violence was required, See Dennis v. United States, 341 U.S. 494 (1951). The Supreme Court ruled that the right to affordable bail after an arrest was essential to Due Process, See Stack v Boyle, 342 U.S. 1 (1951). The Court upheld a conviction of Libel for distributing fliers with "fighting words", See Beauharnais v. Illinois, 343 U.S. 250 (1952). The Court ruled that President Harry S. Truman had exceeded his authority when he ordered seizures of private steel mills during war time for government use, See Youngstown Sheet & Tube Co. v. Sawyer, 343 U.S. 579 (1952). The Jaybird Democratic Association was ruled to be a state actor and was prohibited from excluding Americans from its pre-primary in county elections, See Terry v. Adams, 345 U.S. 461 (1953). Earl Warren was appointed as the Chief Justice in 1953. The Court overruled the separate but equal doctrine, See Brown v. Board of Education of Topeka, 347 U.S. 483 (1954). Th e Court ruled that Congress cannot pass regulations to allow court martial of civilians to be tried in military court, See Kinsella v. Krueger, 354 U.S. 1 (1957). The Supreme Court ruled that the government may not deny passports to citizens suspected of communist Association, See Kent v. Dulles, 357 U.S. 116 (1958). The President may not remove an independent of adjudicatory body without conference of Congress or other personnel outside of the executive branch, See Wiener v. United States, 357 U.S. 349 (1958). Potter Stewart was appointed to The Supreme Court of The United States in 1958. The Court ruled that evidence obtained in violation of the Fourth Amendments guard against unreasonable search and seizure can not be used in state or Federal criminal trial, See Mapp v. Ohio, 367 U.S. 643 (1961). The Court held that constitutional challenges of unequal distribution of voters for legislative seats is an issue the Federal Courts may review, See Baker v. Carr, 369 U.S. 186 (1962). The Supreme Court ruled that the Federal Courts have the authority to provide relief for those detained when the states have failed to do so, See Fay v. Noia, 372 U.S. 391 (1963). The Supreme Court held that it is unconstitutional for a prosecution to withhold exonerating evidence, See Brady v. Maryland, 373 U.S. 83 (1963). The Court ruled that the 1st Amendment protected the press from libel suits and defamatory claims unless an injured party can prove malice or "reckless disregard" for the truth, See New York Times Co. v. Sullivan, 376 U.S. 254 (1964).

The Court eventually began to apply the equal protections to privately owned businesses catering to the public, See Heart of Atlanta Motel, Inc. v. United States, 379 U.S. 241 (1964). The Court ruled all the explicit rights in The Bill of Rights were applicable to all the states, See Malloy v. Hogan, 378 U.S. 1 (1964). The Court overruled the prohibition of contraceptives, See Griswold v. Connecticut, 381 U.S. 479 (1965). The Court affirmed the right to remain silent upon arrest and the right to assistance of counsel in the states, See Miranda v. Arizona, 384 U.S. 436 (1966). The Court struck down state law prohibiting interracial marriage, See Loving v. Virginia, 388 U.S. 1 (1967). The Supreme Court ruled the 1st Amendment does not protect knowingly false media coverage and a trial court should instruct the jury in a defamatory case that plaintiff must show reckless disregard for truth or knowingly presented false coverage, See Time, Inc. v. Hill, 385 U.S. 374 (1967). The Court upheld a conviction based on a search and seizure without probable cause expanding the interpretation of The Fourth Amendment, See Terry v. Ohio, 392 U.S. 1 (1968).The Court affirmed a defendants right to a public jury trial for all crimes and misdemeanors, See Duncan v. Louisiana, 391 U.S. 145 (1968). It was later ruled a tax payer can challenge a Federal or state act which misuses tax money, See Flast v. Cohen, 392 U.S. 83 (1968). The Court ruled government could not regulate speech unless it is "directed to inciting or producing imminent lawless action and is likely to incite or produce such action", See Brandenburg v. Ohio, 395 U.S. 444 (1969). The Court overruled a state requirement of a one year residency to attain welfare benefits, See Shapiro v. Thompson, 394 U.S. 618 (1969). The state law which originated the "fairness doctrine", a requirement mandating broadcasters to consider both sides of an argument and give airtime equally to both sides was upheld and ruled constitutional, See Red Lion Broadcating, Co. v. FCC, 395 U.S. 367 (1969). The Supreme Court overturned another state law being Missouri's redistricting act and the appropriation variances resulting in as little as 1.6% were unconstitutional, See Kirkpatrick v. Preisler, 394 U.S. 526 (1969). Justice Stewart wrote in majority opinion that a warrant-less search upon the arrest of a burglary charge was unreasonable as it was extended beyond the defendants person and area from which he might have obtained either a weapon or something else that could have been used as evidence against him, See Chimel v. California, 395 U.S. 752 (1969). Warren E. Burger was appointed as chief Judge in 1969. The United States Supreme Court ruled there may be a limit on welfare distribution to a single family which causes larger families to receive less money per person than smaller families, See Dandrige v. Williams, 397 U.S. 471 (1970). The Supreme Court ruled that proof beyond a reasonable doubt of every element of a crime was necessary to convict the accused, See In re Winship, 397 U.S. 358 (1970). The Court ruled there was no separate distinction between municipalities and the states and the only separate sovereignties in The United States were the states and The Federal government, See Waller v. Florida, 397 U.S. 387 (1970). A state law which conditioned welfare benefits for U.S. Citizens only was ruled unconstitutional, See Graham v. Richardson, 403 U.S. 365 (1971). The Supreme Court ruled that an insufficient affidavit can not be rehabilitated, See Whiteley v. Warden, 401 U.S. 560 (1971). The Court stressed the constitutional right of interstate travel and upheld a suit alleging the elements or criminal statute 18 U.S.C. § 1985 as a cause of action, See Griffin v. Breckenridge, 403 U.S. 88 (1971). The Supreme Court ruled an obvious unlawful prosecution or prosecution made in bad faith warrants Federal Intervention, See Younger v. Harris, 401 U.S. 37 (1971). The Court ruled that parents are entitled to a neglect hearing when the state attempts to remove non delinquent children from the home for failing to provide suitable care, See Stanley v. Illinois, 405 U.S. 645 (1972). The Court ruled that requiring reporters to testify at a grand jury was not an infringement on The 1st Amendment, See Branzburg v. Hayes, 408 U.S. 665 (1972). Mandatory death penalty sentencing was ruled a violation of The Eighth Amendment without the discretion of a jury, See Furman v. Georgia, 408 U.S. 238 (1972). A Massachusetts law was ruled unconstitutional which prohibited the sale of contraceptives to anyone other than married couples, See Eisenstadt v. Baird, 405 U.S. 438 (1972). The Court affirmed the "established principle that to entitle a private individual to invoke the judicial power to determine the validity of executive or legislative action he must show that he has sustained or is immediately in danger of sustaining a direct injury as the result of that action", See Laird v. Tatum, 408 U.S. 1 (1972); quoting Ex Parte Levitt, 302 U.S. 633 (1937). The Court ruled that a shopping center has the right to prohibit handbill distribution on private property, See Lloyd Corp., Ltd. v. Tanner, 407 U.S. 551 (1972). The Supreme Court wrote in majority opinion the Connecticut pre-garnishment practice was unconstitutional, Justice Stewart wrote "The dichotomy between personal liabilities and property rights is a false one. Property does not have rights. People have rights. The right to enjoy property without unlawful deprivation, no less than the right to speak or the right to travel is in truth a 'Personal' right, whether the 'property' in question be a welfare check, a home, or a savings account.", See Lynch v. Household Finance Corporation, 405 U.S. 538 (1972). The Court ruled the state can not force Amish children to school if it violates their 1st Amendment rights of freedom of religion, See Wisconsin v. Yoder, 406 U.S. 205 (1972). The Supreme Court ruled that a warrantless search of an automobile without probable cause was unconstitutional, See Almeida-Sanchez v. United States, 413 U.S. 266 (1973). The Court determined that the definition of obscenity would be determined not by national standards but by "contemporary community standards", See Miller v. California, 413 U.S. 15 (1973). The Supreme

Court ruled a woman has a constitutional right to have an abortion in the first trimester, See Roe v. Wade, 410 U.S. 113 (1973). The Supreme Court ruled that a pro-se complaint must be liberally construed, See Haines v. Kerner, 404 U.S. 519 (1972). Proof of previous similar conduct to an allegation may corroborate the presumption, See Keyes v. School District No. 1 of Denver, 413 U.S. 189 (1973). When a state official acts in a manner which is violative of the Federal Constitution, that employee is stripped of his official capacity and held subjected to the consequences of his individual Conduct, See Scheuer v. Rhodes, 416 U.S. 232 (1974). The President does not have executive privilege from the orders of The Supreme Court, assuming the orders are constitutional, See U.S. V Nixon, 418 U.S. 683 (1974).The Court upheld an Iowa statute that required residency for a minimum of one year before seeking a divorce in the state courts, See Sosna v. Iowa, 419 U.S. 393 (1975). John Paul Stevens was appointed to the U.S. Supreme Court in 1975. An Oklahoma statute that prohibited the sale of alcohol to males under 21 and girls under 18 was ruled unconstitutional, See Craig v. Boren, 429 U.S. 190 (1976). The Supreme Court upheld the Federal Election Act which has individual contribution limits and a disclosure provision, See Buckley v. Valeo, 424 U.S. 1 (1976). The Social elite and famous are not necessarily considered public figures who assume "any role of especial prominence in the affairs of society", and the standard in a defamation suit for a non-public figure is only a showing of fault, See Time, Inc. v. Firestone, 424 U.S. 448 (1976). The Supreme Court ruled a media preclusion order was unconstitutional, See Nebraska Press Association v. Stuart, 427 US 539 (1976). New Hampshire "live free or die" motto has been published on license plates since, See Wooley v. Maynard, 430 U.S. 705 (1977). The Court upheld warrants for third parties where there is probable cause they posses evidence to a specific crime alleged, See Zurcher v. Stanford Daily, 436 U.S. 547 (1978). The

United States Supreme Court ruled that providing different military benefits to men and women was a violation of equal protections, See Frontiero v. Richardson, 411 U.S. 677 (1978). Regardless of guilt or innocence a person who is deprived of any liberty without a formal hearing which evaluates the evidence from all sides at the standard of probable cause has jurisdiction for an action in law, See Carey v. Piphus, 435 U.S. 247 (1978). The Supreme Court ruled punitive pretrial detainment is unconstitutional as it is a fundamental principle that the accused are innocent until proven guilty, See Bell v. Wolfish, 441 U.S. 520 (1979). The Supreme Court ruled that admissions reserved for minorities was a violation of The Civil Rights Act of 1964, See Regents of The University of California v. Bakke, 438 U.S. 265 (1978). The Supreme Court ruled that disproportionate effects were not sufficient to state a claim and that a showing of intentional discrimination was required , See City of Mobile, Mobile v. Bolden, 446 U.S. 55 (1980).The Court ruled that tax deductions for private or home schooled children was not unconstitutional, See Mueller v. Allen, 463 U.S. 388 (1983). The Supreme Court of The United States ruled that anti discrimination rights were not afforded to gays who could be prosecuted for homosexual activity, See Bowers v. Hardwick, 478 U.S. 186 (1986). The Supreme Court ruled it was constitutional for a commissioned officer not to be able to wear a yarmulke in the military as the military has no obligation to The 1ˢᵗ Amendment, See Goldman v. Weinberger, 475 U.S. 503 (1986). William H. Rehnquist was appointed as Chief Justice in 1986. The Court upheld as constitutional the withholding of federal highway funds from states permitting the purchase of alcohol by persons under 21 years of age. See South Dakota v. Dole, 483 U.S. 203 (1987). The Court ruled that while a person has the right to refuse life sustaining medical treatment, a state may require evidence that a comatose patient would not have wanted to live before withholding treatment, See Cruzan v. Director, Missouri

Department of Health, 497 U.S. 261 (1990). The Court ruled that neither states nor congress could limit terms of congress members because the constitution reserves the right for the people to choose federal lawmakers, See U.S. Term Limits, Inc. Thorton, 514 U.S. 779 (1995). The Court ruled that government programs that classify people by race, unless "narrowly tailored to further "compelling government interests" is unconstitutional, See Adarand Constructors, In. v. Pena, 515 U.S. 200 (1995). The Court ruled that a President does not have immunity from suit for anything outside the official duties of a president, See Clinton v. Jones, 520 U.S. 681 (1997). The Court overruled a portion of a 1993 law banning enforcement of any state law that "substantially burden" religious practices unless there is a "compelling government interest" as an unwarranted infringement upon the Tenth Amendment, See City of Boerne v. Flores, 521 U.S. 507 (1997). The Court set new Guidelines for workplace sexual harassment suits, which allowed employers to be held liable for employee harassment by supervisors, See Faragher v. City of Boca Raton, 524 U.S. 775 (1998). The Supreme Court prohibited statistical sampling in appointing seats in the U.S. House, requiring a head count to made, See Department of Commerce v. U.S. House of Representatives, 525 U.S. 316 (1999). The Supreme Court upheld as constitutional the right to dismiss an association member for being a homosexual by vote, See Boy Scouts of America v. Dale, 530 U.S. 640 (2000). The Supreme Court ruled that recounts of the 2000 Florida ballots, could not continue due to inconsistent evaluations that violated the equal protection clause, the effect was the existing official results would stand making George w. Bush the marginal election winner, See Bush v. Gore, 531 U.S. 98 (2000). The Supreme Court ruled in a split decision that it is illegal for law enforcement to scan a person's home with thermal imaging without a warrant, See Kyllo v. United States, 533 U.S. 27 (2001). The Court ruled that a strict point system based on applicants racial background was unconstitutional for The University of Michigan Law School admission process, See Gratz v. Bollinger, 539 U.S. 244 (2003). The Court ruled that the disabled could sue the states under the Americans with disabilities Act of 1990, See Tennessee v. Lane, 541 U.S. 509 (2004). The Court struck down federal legislation passed in 1998 to restrict online access of adult media on the basis that it violated The First Amendment, See Ashcroft v. American Civil Liberties Union, 542 U.S. 656 (2004). The Court ruled that local governments could force property owners to sell their land in order to facilitate private development projects expected to benefit the community, See Kelo v. City of New London, 545 U.S. 469 (2005). John G. Roberts was appointed as Chief Justice in 2005. The Supreme Court ruled the 1st Amendment does not protect from liability public employees who make statements of slander, See Garcetti v. Ceballos, 547 U.S. 410 (2006). The Court ruled that President Bush's system trying terrorism detainees at the U.S. Military base in Guantanamo Bay was unauthorized under federal law and the International Geneva Conventions, See Hamdan v. Rumsfeld, 548 U.S. 557 (2006). The Supreme Court upheld an Indiana law requiring voters to present a valid government form of photo identification, See Crawford v. Marion County Election Board, 553 U.S. 181 (2008). The Court ruled that even a president can be a respondent to a Habeas Corpus, See Boumediene v. Bush, 553 U.S. 723 (2008). The United States Supreme Court overruled D.C.'s hand gun ban as a violation of The 2nd Amendment, See District of Columbia v. Heller, 554 U.S. 570 (2008). The Supreme Court ruled that federal law prohibiting corporations from using general funds to finance campaign advertisements was unconstitutional, See Citizens United v. Federal Election Commission, 558 U.S. 310 (2010). The Supreme Court ruled that placing a GPS tracking device on someones vehicle was unconstitutional without a warrant, See United States v. Jones, 565 U.S. 400 (2012). The Court ruled that police need a warrant to search a person's cell phone, See Riley v. California, 573 U.S. 373 (2014). The Court ruled in a split decision that state statues banning same sex marriage were unconstitutional, See Obergefell v. Hodges, 576 U.S. 644 (2015). The Supreme Court ruled that Texas abortion law was too restrictive and placed an undue burden on women, See Whole Woman's Health v. Hellerstedt, 579 U.S. __ (2016). The Supreme Court of The United States ruled a criminal defendant may bring a claim under The Fourth Amendment to challenge pretrial confinement, See Manuel v. City of Joliet, Ill., 580 S. Ct. 911 (2017). The Supreme Court ruled that a union could not require non-union members to pay union fees, See Janus v. American Federation of State, County and Municipal Employees, 585 U.S. __ (2018). The Supreme Court ruled that The U.S. Courts have no authority to stop block partisan gerrymandering, See Rucho v. Common Cause, 588 U.S. __ (2019).

CHAPTER 10

The Declaration of Independence is the first legal document forming our country. It was drafted by Thomas Jefferson and revised by the Continental Congress. It contains erratic capitalizations. It is a truly amazing document that embodies natural law and the purpose of life. "We hold these truths to be self-evident, that all men are created equal, that they are endowed by their Creator with certain unalienable Rights, that among these are Life, Liberty and the pursuit of Happiness." and "That to secure these rights, Governments are instituted among Men, deriving their just powers from the consent of the governed, = That whenever any Form of Government becomes destructive of these ends, it is the Right of the People to alter or to abolish it, and to institute new Government, laying its foundation on such principles and organizing its powers in such form, as to them shall seem most likely to effect their Safety and Happiness.", See The Declaration of Independence. It then proceeds to list a number of reasons the colonies demanded to be "absolved from all Allegiance to the British Crown". Of these reasons was that of "arbitrary government" and that the King of England had "sent hither Swarms of Officers to harass our people". The writers also stated, "For transporting us beyond Seas to be tried for pretend Offenses". That's right, we fought a war for independence from a country which charged people for "pretend Offenses". The world has seen it before, it was happening around the world long before our country was even founded. Law enforcement has been unlawfully prosecuting people probably since the beginning of law enforcement. The Declaration of Independence the states, "A Prince, whose character is thus marked by every act which may define a Tyrant, is unfit to be the Ruler of a free People".

Article V of The United States Constitution enables three quarters of state legislators to call for a state convention upon which three quarters of those who attend the convention may ratify amendments to to The U.S. Constitution. Article V states: "Whenever two thirds of both houses shall deem it necessary, shall propose amendments to this constitution, or, on the application of the legislators of two thirds of the several states, shall call a convention for proposing amendments, which, in either case, shall be valid to all intents and purposes, as part of this constitution, when ratified by the legislators of three fourths of the several states, or by the conventions in three fourths thereof". This means the states have the authority to pass a legal revolution with or without the Federal Government. "We need a revolution every 200 years, because all governments become stale and corrupt after 200 years"= Benjamin Franklin. There needs to be a massive recession by the Federal government regardless, whether through a state convention, Congressional Act or from internal executive orders, See Humphrey's Executor v. United States, 295 U.S. 602 (1935). Pro-rated pensions should be offered immediately to those who's jobs are terminated. Retrogression must begin immediately. We are are almost thirty trillion in debt. I suggest passing an amendment that limits government service, except the military and judicial branches, to a maximum of eight years. It would take take about eight years to balance the budget if the United States government completely shut down. Active duty military can be transferred to The National Guard or reserves, most of the executive branch may retire with benefits, the unaffordable Health Car Act must be repealed and at least half the federal government should be on indefinite leave with benefits. The new objective should be the balance the budget and mitigate the debt. The objective should be efficiency. "We, the people are rightful masters of both Congress and the courts – not to overthrow the Constitution, but to overthrow the men who pervert the Constitution."= Abraham Lincoln.

The Five Worst Supreme Court of the United States Rulings. The Supreme Court changed the standard for Civil Proceedings from "possible" to "plausible", Stevens and Ginsberg Dissented, See Bell Atlantic Corp. v. Twombly, 550 U.S. 544 (2007). The Supreme Court ruled a judge was not in in "clear absence of all jurisdiction" after having ordered the sterilization of a fifteen year old girl, Judge Stewart wrote in Dissent "But the scope of judicial immunity is limited to liability for "judicial acts," and I think that what Judge Stump did on July 9, 1971, was beyond the pale of anything that could sensibly be called a judicial act", Marshall, Powell and Stewart Dissented, See Stump v. Sparkman, 435 U.S. 349 (1978). The Supreme Court lowered the standard of evidence to "reasonable suspicion" for a certain types of searches, Dissent by Douglas, See Terry v. Ohio, 392 U.S. 1 (1968). The Supreme Court accepted as the basis for probable cause an anonymous letter,

Steven, Brennan and Marshall Dissented, See Illinois v. Gates, 462 U.S. 213 (1983). The Supreme Court ruled the use of a PIT(Precision Intervention Technique) was Constitutional, Dissented by Stevens, See Scott v. Harris, 550 U.S. 372 (2007).

The Holy Bible says "Be fruitful and increase in number", See Genesis: 1:28. The two-witness rule is in The Holy Bible, "One witness is not enough to convict anyone accused of any crime or offense they may have committed. A matter must be established by the testimony of two or three witnesses.", See Deuteronomy 19:15. The Old Testament is at least two thousand years old. If police today followed the wisdom of the Bible's restrictions on arrests I never would have been arrested in the first place. Here it is again, "Anyone who kills a person is to be put to death as a murderer only on the testimony of witnesses. But no one is to be put to death on the testimony of only one witness.", See Numbers 35:30. Compensatory/punitive damages are in The Holy Bible, "Whoever steals an ox or a sheep and slaughters it or sells it must pay back five head of cattle for the ox and four sheep for the sheep.", See Exodus 22. Malicious prosecutions are in The Holy Bible, "Do not spread false reports. Do not help a guilty person by being a malicious witness.", See Exodus 23. Kidnapping is a capitol offense in The Bible, "Anyone who kidnaps someone is to be put to death, whether the victim has been sold or is still in the kidnapper's possession.", See Exodus 21:16. "Do not deny justice to your poor people in their lawsuits. Have nothing to do with a false charge and do not put an innocent or honest person to death, for I will not acquit the guilty.", See Exodus 23:6. False allegations are in The Ten Commandments, "You shall not give false testimony against your neighbor.", See Deuteronomy 5:20. The corruption of the judicial system is in The Holy Bible, "Appoint judges and officials for each of your tribes in every town the Lord your God has given you, and they shall judge the people fairly. Do not pervert justice or show partiality. Do not accept a bribe, for a bribe blinds the eyes of the wise and twists the words of the innocent. Follow justice and justice alone, so that you may live and possess the land the Lord your God is giving you.", See Deuteronomy 16:18. The Holy Bible also states, "If a man has sexual relations with a man as one does with a woman, both of them have done what is detestable. They are to be put to death; their blood will be on their own heads.", See Leviticus 20:13.

In regards to the role of the U.S. Government it is essential to discern necessity from opinion and keep the later out of law. The federal government is bound to the U.S. Constitution and The Declaration of Independence. "We the people" in the preamble means a citizen's perspective comes before government's. No court ruling or legislation can overrule The Declaration of Independence and The U.S. Constitution or the grammatical inferences of the explicit rights declared therein. The U.S. Government is bound to the preamble of The Constitution which states: "We the People of the United States, in Order to form a more perfect Union, establish Justice, insure domestic Tranquility, provide for the common defense, promote the general Welfare, and secure the Blessings of Liberty to ourselves and our Posterity, do ordain and establish this Constitution for the United States of America". The law of The Constitution takes precedent over other law, whether congressional or state. The Hierarchy of Law is The Declaration of Independence and U.S. Constitution, U.S. Supreme court Law, Congressional Law Then State Supreme court Law, State legislative law then local ordinances.

Rule 12(b)(6) of the Federal Rules of Civil Procedure dismissals are a big problem, stating "failure to state a claim upon which relief can be granted". This often premature dismissal prevents the case from proceeding through discovery and even prevents the defendants from their otherwise obligation to respond to the allegations. This is civil justice we are talking about. For instance most of the lawsuits I filed in Arizona during my detainment were dismissed by Rule 12(b)(6) and despite having very valid claims and a lot of evidence the defendants were not even required to admit or deny the allegations. This is a form of law enforcement and it in no way benefits society to dismiss claims of unconstitutional conduct without proceeding through discovery. In one of the worst rulings of all time by The Supreme Court of The United States they overruled the previous evidentiary standard that "a complaint should not be dismissed for failure to state a claim unless it appears beyond doubt that the plaintiff can prove no set of facts in support of his claim which would entitle him to relief", See Conley v. Gibson, 355 U.S. 41 (1957)(Unanimous Decision); See also Haines v. Kerner, 404 U.S. 519 (1972) and replaced it with the requirement of "only enough facts to state a claim to relief that is plausible on its face", See Bell Atlantic Corp. v. Twombly, 550 U.S. 544 (2007). The standard was once "conceivable" and is now "plausible". Justice Stevens filed a dissenting opinion with which Justice Ginsburg joined. This made civil litigation between private parties and especially against the government more difficult. In this case William Twombly and Lawrence Marcus filed a class action lawsuit against Bell Atlantic and a number of other telecommunications companies alleging they were in violation of §1 of the Sherman Antitrust Act which makes monopolistic behavior illegal. The U.S. District court dismissed the claim for " failure to state a claim upon which relief can be granted" pursuant Fed. R. Civ. P. Rule 12(b)(6) and the U.S. Court of Appeals 2nd Circuit reversed. The Supreme Court of The United States reversed the decision of the Court of Appeals and supported the dismissal. In addition to creating a major obstacle in the way of civil justice the court sent the wrong message regarding corporate monopolies. As Justice Stevens pointed out in a case of an alleged violation of the Sherman Act, it was especially important that the case proceed through discovery. Once, I googled as many corporations as I could think of and found every corporation had a parent corporation. These parent corporations often had more parent corporations and It appeared as if there were likely numerous violations of the Sherman Antitrust Act.

Free elections need to be exercised on all levels of governments, state and federal. Legislators should have term limits, no one in government should serve more than eight years of public service. Staying in office forever prevents the healthy cycle of elections necessary to maintain true democracy and republic. College Graduates should serve one year of paid internship in government of their choice and the government should make this easy and accessible for applicants. The government is not separate from the public, the government is public. Law enforcement and other bureaucrats spending their entire life in government is making the government less of a public entity. This is public service, bureaucrat's careers come second to the interests of the public. They should seek a state level law enforcement position after serving eight years in the U.S. Government. The Media should be covering elections as the highest of priorities and citizens should be invited to public events on a regular basis. Ask ten random people if they know how to run as a state legislator, ask them if they know a state legislator, ask them when the next state or local assembly is, ask them if they know how their state government works. This is a pragmatic knowledge that should be a prerequisite to graduating high school as should intro courses to constitutional law, civil litigation and criminal law. State departments especially police departments should have citizen committees to approve applicants after meeting them in person, serving at most two year terms with a max term limit of two terms and they shall meet every two to six months or however often be necessary. This will ensure the employment of representatives who have the best interests for then public and everyone will know they were only employed because the public wanted them to be. Our Constitution secures infinite right of opportunity to every person in this country regardless of race or gender. The more we deviate from the law of The Constitution the more we risk an excessive and unstable U.S. Government. In 2009 we spent over 160% of the federal budget and are now over 28 trillion dollars in debt. Bush Balanced the budget however, he failed to maintain and enforce the constitution within the states by making enough prosecutions under The Civil Rights Act. The federal top priority should be to ensure out of state resident's U.S. Constitutional rights are protected in any state they may travel. Diversity Jurisdiction for residents from another state codifies exactly that, See 28 U.S.C. §1332; Wagenmann v. Adams, 829 F.2d 196 (1st Cir. 1987). If the federal government can't uphold this duty than they obviously something needs to change. I posted a fifteen minute lecture on YouTube in December 2017 regarding the "right and duty" to "reinstate" the government as described in the Declaration of Independence. I suggest entirely lawful means of a legislative revolution with an Article V Convention. In late 2017 I sent letters to all fifty governors to be forwarded to the legislators and I asked to meet with them regarding an Article V convention.

The President like a governor or mayor, has the absolute right to remove officials from office who are under their executive authority. They can fire an employee for any reason other than to act in a conspiracy. They can and should purge employees for conduct complaints and misdemeanor convictions that wouldn't necessarily mandate termination. Executive officials don't however exercise this right very often due to pressures from law enforcement and police unions. This rule was affirmed by The Supreme Court of The United States, See Humphrey's Executor v. United States, 295 U.S. 602 (1935). How is it even possible, so many obscene constitutional violations by state law enforcement. The Oath of

The President states, "I do solemnly swear (or affirm) that I will faithfully execute the Office of President of the United States, and will to the best of my Ability, preserve, protect and defend the Constitution of the United States.", See Article II §1. Every judicial and executive officer in this country is required to take an oath to support The U.S. Constitution, See Article VI §3. The entire U.S. Department of justice was built to enforce the Civil Rights Act however they don't enforce it as they should. "It is the duty of courts to be watchful for the constitutional rights of the citizen, and against any stealthy encroachments thereon.", See Boyd v. United States, 116 U.S. 616 (1886).

The first homo sapiens appeared around 300 thousand years ago. Our oldest fossils date back to around this time in Morocco. The earliest cave paintings found are from around 32 thousand years ago in Sulawesi, Indonesia and Cosquer and Chauvet in Southern France. The Denisovans are the earliest known peoples around 50 thousand years ago. Neanderthals even prior to the first homo Sapiens were already using tools made of bone and bi facially flaked Stone. The oldest written records in history were found in Mesopotamia about 4000 BCE in The Tigris-Euphrates River valley. The Early European Minoan civilization emerged around 2,500 BCE with a healthy economy and decorative arts, trading with other cities of the Mediterranean sea including Mycenae of Greece, and Troy of Asia Minor among others. The First Laws of the Amorites were codified by Hammurabi around 1775 BCE. Which had biblical parallels. The Phoenician alphabet was designed around 1600 BCE. The Aegean area saw a rich elaboration on intellectual life and Arts, Philosophy of Plato, Socrates and Aristotle advocating "rational idealism" developed around 400 BCE. Democracy became practice in Athens, Greece around this time, Architecture, Poetry, Drama and the Olympics developed around this time. Hellenistic Philosophy stressed the importance of a persons search for happiness while the Zeno and Stoics honored Logic and Reason. The epicureans tried to build lives of moderate pleasure without political or emotional involvement. The City of Rome was founded around 750 BCE where Latin and the Aristocratic original republic government was later developed along with Roman Law including the practice of trial by jury. There was a scientific revolution especially in Alexandria, Egypt where the Ptolemies furnished a great library and museum. The Study of Mathematics developed with the Study of Euclid Geometry, Astronomy with the heliocentric theory of Aristarchus , geography with the world map of Eratosthenes, hydraulics with Archimedes, the Julian calendar, Ptolemy's Almagest all between 300 -45 BCE. A school for Priests was established in Alexandria. In Rome the study of theology and law was established at the Academy of Yavneh where debates regarding ethics, Law, liturgy, rulings, biblical exegesis, and historic materials succeeded. By the 1st Century missionary activities of the christian Apostles such as Paul of Tarsus, spread the faith. Under the Roman Ruler Constantine (306-337) Christianity became the established religion of the empire. Pagan worship was banned by the end of the Fourth Century. Germanic troops and commanders dominated the Roman armies by 500 CE. St. Patrick completed Irish Conversion to Christianity (457-492) where a strong tradition originated. Irish monastic missionaries later helped restore Christianity in Scotland and England (521-597) where the Pre-Roman Celtic culture then remained. The Byzantine Empire followed the Roman Empire and under Justinian (527-565) temporarily conquered parts of Spain, North Africa and Italy codifying Roman Law. Danish and Norse Scandinavian Pagans or Vikings raided the coasts of the British Isles, France and The Mediterranean for over 200 years beginning in the 8th Century. The first English King Egbert, King of Wessex rule began in 829. The German Kingdom which had been comprised of mainly autonomous states formed the Holy Roman Empire in which Italy was ruled by Germany (936-1250). Pope Urban II called for a crusade in 1095 to restore Asia Minor to Byzantium and the Holy land to Christendom. Guilds dominated much of factory textile production and agricultural economy. The Magna Carta was granted by King John to the rebellious Barons in 1215. The Black Death also known as the Bubonic Plague struck Europe killing almost half of the population (1348-1350). The Scientific revolution began around 1300 where neo-thinkers Paris and Oxford challenged previous orthodox. Copernicus (1475-1543), Kepler (1571-1630) described mathematical laws describing planetary orbits. Galileo Galileo (1564-1642) found moving sun spots, irregular moon topography and moons around Jupiter, with Sir. Isaac Newton (1642-1716) they solved significant planetary phenomena, Leibniz (1646-1716) invented calculus, Rene Descartes (1596-1650) known for his influential philosophy invented analytic geometry, Leeuwenhoek (1632-1723) discovered microscopic life, Harvey (1578-1657) studied blood circulation, Boyle (1627-1691) studied chemistry, Vesalius (1514-1564) advanced anatomy. Thomas Savery invented the steam engine which he presented to the London Royal Society in1698. The revolution of the Arts occurred in the 1500 and 1600s. The power of reason and empirical observation was stressed by Francis Bacon (1561-1626). A system of rationalistic philosophy calling for political and intellectual freedom was found in the work "Ethics" by Spinoza (1632-1677). Emigration to North America began in the 1500s.

For-profit postsecondary education systems in the united states have very high student loan default rates. Previous regulations on for-profit institutions were repealed by the Bush administration. Under Obama the Gainful Employment Rule was enacted in 2014 which limited financial aid to students attending schools with a poor debt to earnings ratio of graduates. This bankrupt Corinthian Colleges which was the second largest for-profit college chain in the country. The Gainful

Employment Rule was repealed in 2019 under Donald Trump who himself was a defendant in a number of lawsuits alleging fraud against Trump University. It has created a free-for-all of predatory for-profit schools that use less than ethical recruitment tactics. Many for-profit institutions have been exposed as providing poor education, having high tuition rates and often providing degrees that aren't recognized by their industries, See the documentary *Fail State* (2017).

Christopher Columbus first sighted North American Land in 1492. The first two settlements were San Miguel de Guadalupe for the summer of 1526 and a two year colony on Paris Island starting in 1562, both were off the coast of South Carolina. St. Augustine, Florida was founded in 1565 and has remained until present day. Sir Francis Drake in 1579 claimed San Fransisco Bay and the region for Britain. Roanoke Island, North Carolina was first settled in 1585 by Sir Walter Raleigh. James Town, Virginia was founded in 1607 by Capt. John Smith. Manhattan was bought from the Manhatta Indians for $24 in 1626. Maryland was founded by Lord Baltimore as a Catholic colony in 1634. Providence, Road Island and Harvard College were founded in 1636. The *Pilgrim's Progress* by John Bunyan was published in 1681. El Paso, Texas was settled by The Spanish in 1682. The First colonial newspaper, the *Public Occurrences* was published by Benjamin Harris who also Published the *England Primer* in 1689. William Kidd was hung for conspiracy in 1699. The newspaper, *Boston News Letter*, was first published in 1704. The first theater opened in Williamsburg, Virginia in 1716. Benjamin Franklin published *Poor Richards Almanac* in 1732. A cast of Liberty Bell was delivered from England to Pennsylvania in 1752. The French and Indian war began and Benjamin Franklin proposed a plan for union of the states in 1754. The first streetlights were built in Philadelphia. British troops fired into crowd killing five which was later called the Boston Massacre in 1770. Patrick Henry gave speech to the Virginia Convention at

St. John's Church in Richmond, Virginia for preparation in war, "Gentlemen may cry peace, peace but there is no peace. The War has actually begun! The next gale that sweeps from the north will bring to our ears the clash of resounding arms! Our brethren are already in the field! Why stand we here idle? What is it that gentlemen wish? What would they have? Is life so dear, or peace so sweet, as to be purchased at the price of chains and slavery? Forbid it. Almighty God! I know not what course others may take: but as for me, give me liberty, or give me death!", given March 23rd, 1775. The Declaration of Independence was signed July 4th in 1776 and The War for Independence continued until The Treaty of Paris in 1783. State delegates asked for a constitutional convention in 1786. George Washington was chosen President 1789. The First U.S. Supreme Court session was held in NYC February 2nd 1790. The Bill of Rights went into effect September 25th 1789. Western Pennsylvania farmers protested liquor taxes in The Whiskey Rebellion in 1794. General Wayne signed The Treaty of Greenville with the Midwest Indians in 1795. John Adams became the second President in 1797. U.S. Government moved to Washington D.C. In 1800. Thomas Jefferson became President in 1801. Alexander Hamilton was shot and killed by Aaron Burr in a duel in 1804. The Embargo Act prohibited trade with all foreign countries in 1807. Legislation outlawing the import of slaves goes into effect in 1808. James Madison became President in 1809. Hundreds of slaves revolted in Louisiana, seventy five were killed in 1811. War was declared with Britain after seizing U.S. ships trading with France in 1812. U.S. won Battle of Lake Erie and Battle of the Thames in 1813. British defeated U.S. Troops in Maryland and burned The Capitol and White House in 1814. Peace treaty with Britain signed December 24th 1814. British troops unaware of the treaty attacked U.S. Troops near New Orleans and suffered more than 2,000 casualties, U.S. lost 71 in 1815. The American Colonization Society which sought to transport freed blacks to Africa was formed in 1816. James Monroe became President in 1817. Connecticut then Massachusetts and New York expanded voting rights to white males by reducing or eliminating property qualifications, 1818-1821. Spain surrendered Florida to The United States in 1819. The first organized factory strike in the U.S. was the Weavers Strike in 1824. John Quincy Adams became President in 1825. Massachusetts became the first state to have public high schools in 1827. Noah Webster published the *American Dictionary of the English Language* and the first passenger railroad began operation in 1828. Andrew Jackson became President in 1829. Nat Turner was hanged for leading a local slave rebellion in 1831. Black Hawk War pushed Indians west of Mississippi River in 1832. Oberlin College became the first university to adopt coeducation in 1833. The Florida Seminole Indians protested forced removal in 1835. Texans were surrounded by Mexicans and killed in The Battle of Alamo in 1836. Cherokee Indians walked the "Trail of Tears" in 1838. First wagon train departed Independence, Missouri for California in 1841. The Webster-Ashburton Treaty between The United States and The British North American Colonies was signed in 1842. The first successful telegraph message was sent from inventor Samuel F.B. Morse in Washington D.C. to Baltimore in 1844. The first time Congress overrode a President's veto was in 1845. The Mexican war was in 1846. Henry Wadsworth Longfellow published the work *Evangeline* in 1847. The first Women's Rights Convention was held in Seneca Falls, New York in 1848. California was admitted to union and *The Scarlet Letter* was published in 1850. Treaty was signed to open trade with Japan and Stephen Foster published *My Old Kentucky Home* in 1853. The Republican Party is formed in Wisconsin and Henry David Thoreau published *Walden* in 1854. First railroad train west of the Mississippi River was in 1855. The Lincoln-Douglas debates were in 1858. Abolitionists took control of a U.S. Armory at Harpers Ferry, West Virginia in

1859. Shoe workers went on strike throughout New England in the country's largest strike to date in 1860. The start of the Civil War with the First Battle of Bull Run was in 1861. The Homestead Act was passed giving away free land to settlers in 1862.

On March 25th 1931 a fight broke out on a train traveling through Alabama between seven white men and nine African Americans. Six of the seven white men were thrown from the train. Two white women remained on the train who claimed they had been raped. The white men reported the fight to authorities and and a sheriff deputized a posse comitatus and arrested the nine defendants and two others in Paint rock, Alabama after stopping the train. The defendants were taken to Scottsboro, Alabama where they were met by an angry white mob of thousands. The sheriff had to call the National Guard to defend the prisoners. The trials began April 6th less than two weeks after the arrests. The nine defendants were tried in in four groups of 2,1,5 and 1 defendants. Alabama law provided the sentence was to be determined by the jury and ranged from ten years to death. All defendants except the last were convicted and sentenced to death. Three of the defendants, who testified to their own innocence, stated they saw others accused commit the crime. The defendants later known as the "Scottsboro Boys" were described as "ignorant and illiterate" by The Supreme Court of The United states who reversed their convictions and ordered new trials on the grounds that they were denied "effective" assistance of counsel in violation of due process of law. On remand the defendants were convicted again and sentenced to death. The trial judge granted motions for new trials and the defendants were convicted a third time however the convictions were again overturned by The Supreme Court of the United States for systematically excluding African-Americans from the jury. Four of the nine defendants were eventually able to get their charges dropped. Only one of the five received the death penalty a fourth time but was commuted to life imprisonment by the Alabama Governor. One of the men plead guilty to assaulting a deputy and served twenty years in prison and another escaped in 1948. In 2013 the state of Alabama passed historic legislation exonerating all nine defendants. All the remaining defendants served lengthy prison sentences, See Powell v. Alabama, 287 U.S. 45 (1932); Norris v. Alabama, 294 U.S. 587 (1935); Patterson v. Alabama, 294 U.S. 600 (1935).

CHAPTER 11

The left wants to implement a totalitarian government that would defy the purpose of life. They practice what's called "cancel culture" and seem to believe in preventing their opposition from expressing their views. This is what they did in Arizona and it's what they did to Donald Trump and Jordan Peterson who have been censored on social media. Our country was founded on principals of Freedom of Speech and this mentality is a disgrace. The other thing the democrats do is hold an ideal and cling to a false sense the moral superiority. The only Utopia is a Limited government with maximum liberty. These views are superficial reflecting a shallow base of knowledge and do not reflect the study of law, principle or fact. It is morally superior to defend Liberty, individualism, exceptionalism and equal protections of Law. Liberty equates to a person's right to fulfill their purpose in life whatever that may be and Pursuit of Happiness. Restrictions on Liberty and Freedom of Speech is NOT the answer. Big government is dangerous. The democrats seem to want to make white people a second class citizen in this country. Every day is a battle to prevent our country of infinite opportunity and equal protections of law from becoming a police state dystopia. The Democrats also want to end the right of parents to home school their children so the children can be mind controlled and so the liberals can suppress conservative teachings. The democratic policies are pandering with short-sighted goals. They obviously seek to buy votes with government benefits especially since The Recovery Act in 2009 when they started giving away stimulus checks. It's an uphill battle for conservatives after the liberals robbed the tax payers and started giving away free stuff. I'm tired of hearing about racism after having a half black President. Racism does not exist to the extent that it would prevent upward mobility, professional success and pursuit of happiness. I believe in equal opportunity and equal protections of law however the idea of equality beyond that is preposterous. This is the land of infinite opportunity and would not be what it is if the government was bottle feeding tens of millions of people. Differences in IQ and work ethic are always going to be major factors in success. Racism isn't the problem. The courts encourage racism as they provide additional protections for those who are prejudiced for reasons of race in violation of the Fourteenth Amendment. It is not required that a person's constitutional violations be for racial reasons to be afforded protections under the Civil Rights Act but it helps. Therefore every time something happens to a person of color, it's because their black. A lawless criminal justice system however is the problem. More unarmed white men are killed every year by police than unarmed African-Americans but we rarely hear about that. More white people are killed by black people than black killed by white people and those who claim systemic racism have clearly overlooked this fact. Racism is over represented. It also is a distraction from the central issues we face together. Black Lives Matter would appear less racist if they would advocate for the constitutional rights of all people and unilaterally against all unlawful conduct by police. They should just argue that we have a homicidal police problem. Everything revolves around race for them. That's racist. The argument of systemic racism is about power by use of white guilt and reverse discrimination. Lets not forget this country fought a war and those who believe everyone must be equal in the eyes of the law won. Many lives were lost fighting a war to help African-Americans. People today don't owe African Americans anything other than equal protections of law like everybody else. I do however agree that police should be defunded for illegal use of deadly force and other unlawful conduct. There are many people with Masters Degrees making what police in the Cities make. When you factor in the pensions and see that government employees are actually making two to three times their salary and most with about six months of training one might wonder why anyone would tolerate any illegal behavior. They will continue to push for an expansion of power unless the public pushes back. I say hell ya defund the police if they violate anyone's Rights. Although there are probably better solutions than defunding an entire department. Police should all wear cameras and could drive slow cars and be unarmed like they are in Europe. I also agree with progressive taxes and think Trump's proposal for those who make under $25,000 per year to pay no federal income tax is brilliant. Make it under $30k per year, $60k for couples. This is a very logical way to help the underprivileged by encouraging them to work and help their efforts go further. It is such a good idea it makes democratic policies look insane. Most democrats are completely unaware their candidates propose tax increases for everyone including those who can't pay their bills or they wouldn't vote for democratic candidates. I support a 12% corporate tax rate like Reagan. I also believe global warming is probably real, See *The Island President* (2011) and *An Inconvenient Sequel: Truth to Power* (2017). If you have ever supported democratic policies read "*Live Free or Die*" by Sean Hannity. I've read *A Promise Land* by

Barrack Obama and the way he beats around the bush is ridiculous. Furthermore taxes should not be raised because that would encourage individuals and corporations to leave the country and take their business elsewhere which is very bad for GDP and the economy. Until recently the U.S. Had one of the highest corporate taxes in the world. I am generally pro immigration but think a felony conviction should result in deportation. "Sanctuary Cities" should not be accommodating lawfully convicted felons. You'll notice the conservatives can talk for hours passionately about their beliefs while the democrats have a short pitch. I think the affordable Health Care Act should be repealed. The last thing we needed was to mix the medical industry with the inefficiencies and incompetence of government. I think unified health care is dangerous because it's very important that people be able to get different independent opinions. Conservative radio hosts can speak endlessly about law and statistics because their arguments make sense and are connected to facts and truth. The democrats on the other hand tend to make small talk because their arguments are flawed. I do however also agree with the movement to decriminalize illicit drugs. There is a balance between individualism and absolute democracy. In the United States the Constitution requires that we put individuals rights above absolute democracy. This protects the millionaires and billionaires from a majority that would steal everything from them. The far left policies are parasitic. The lawless conduct of the government in these cases are proof we already have a problem with excessive government. The unlawful arrests, the prosecutions and the detainment. The government is too big and public employees are not afraid of being prosecuted. It's frustrating when I speak to people who have blind trust in the government and don't understand we already have a problem. The central issue we should be addressing is law enforcement's lack of respect for human dignity and the civil rights of all people.

In 1986 The Supreme Court of The United States ruled that a Georgia statute that prohibited homosexual sodomy between consenting adults was constitutional. "After being charged with violating the Georgia statute criminalizing sodomy by committing that act with another adult male in the bedroom of his home, respondent Hardwick (respondent) brought suit in Federal District Court, challenging the constitutionality of the statute insofar as it criminalized consensual sodomy. The court granted the defendants' motion to dismiss for failure to state a claim. The Court of Appeals reversed and remanded, holding that the Georgia statute violated respondent's fundamental rights.". The Supreme Court of The United States however ruled, "The Constitution does not confer a fundamental right upon homosexuals to engage in sodomy.". The Court also stated, "Sodomy was a criminal offense at common law and was forbidden by the laws of the original 13 States when they ratified the Bill of Rights." and "until 1961, all 50 States outlawed sodomy, and today, 24 States and the District of Columbia continue to provide criminal penalties for sodomy performed in private and between consenting adults.". Chief Justice Burger stated in concurring opinion, "Homosexual sodomy was a capitol crime under Roman Law... To hold that the act of homosexual sodomy is somehow protected as a fundamental right would be to cast aside millennia of moral teaching.", See Bowers v Hardwick, 478 U.S. 186 (1986). This decision was overruled in 2003, "If I were a member of the Texas Legislature, I would vote to repeal it. Punishing someone for expressing his sexual preference through noncommercial consensual conduct with another adult does not appear to be a worthy way to expend valuable law enforcement resources.", See Lawrence v. Texas, 539 U.S. 558 (2003)(Thomas, Dissenting). Man evolved of hundreds of thousands of years and made homosexuality illegal a few thousand years ago, then in 2003 the U.S. Supreme Court forced every city and state in the country to accept homosexuality into their community in possible the worst ruling of all time. We now have a conservative Supreme Court of The United States and this must be overruled. As Judge Thomas suggested in Dissent this issue should be left for the states to decide. Many homosexuals can't relate to straight men and don't understand the principals of self defense or stand your ground laws because they are among the parasites that harass the straight men. They feel they have failed at being a man and sometimes secretly want others to fail too. Homosexuals just degrade each other then start trying to degrade straight men if they have the power. The DSM (Diagnostic and Statistical Manual of Mental Disorders) used to classify homosexuality as a mental disorder. Could the legalization of homosexuality eventually lead to straight people being treated like they are the one's with a mental disorder? Homosexuality seems to be spreading at an alarming rate. A very important question everyone should be asking is whether or not homosexuals statistically are more likely to be criminals and the answer is yes much more likely. They intentionally go to jail where there are no women. Their typical backwards, reckless and shallow political beliefs could create a dystopia so disrespectful it's worse than death. Particularly the liberal assault on Freedom of Speech, education, high taxes, health care and forced injections and mask mandates. Many liberal policies are entirely counterproductive to purpose of life. Some people believe they are controlled by aliens that make them act unnatural and would end the World if they had any power. The world depends upon Men who do the right thing, can't be controlled and don't back down.

In 1973 The Supreme Court of The United States ruled in a 7-2 decision that the prohibition of first term abortions was unconstitutional. The court ruled, "For the stage subsequent to approximately the end of the first trimester, the State, in promoting its interest in the health of the mother, may, if it chooses, regulate the abortion procedure in ways that are reasonably related to maternal health" and "For the stage subsequent to viability the State, in promoting its interest in the potentiality of human life, may, if it chooses, regulate, and even proscribe, abortion except where necessary, in appropriate medical judgment, for the preservation of the life or health of the mother". This case based its conclusion primarily on a woman's "Right of Privacy", See Roe v. Wade, 410 U.S. 113 (1973). This case initiated years of political debate on abortion. I think abortions should be strongly discouraged but should ultimately up to the states. A recent split decision The U.S. Supreme Court upheld a Texas statute that prevents abortion after six weeks, See Whole Woman's Health et al. *v.* Austin Reeve Jackson, Judge, et al., 594 U. S. ___ (2021). This ruling will allow other states if their elected representatives choose to prohibit abortion as early as six weeks. This was a tremendous achievement for conservatives after Trump appointed three judges to the court.

Portugal, a country of over 10,000,000 decriminalized all illicit drugs in 2001. It has now been proven that money is more effectively spent providing addiction treatment centers, than it is criminally prosecuting people and imprisoning them. Users with no more than a ten day supply can be given citations and required to be seen before a commission composed of a social worker, a psychiatrist, and an attorney. The commission can impose therapy or community service. A former constitutional court judge Rui Pereira, was of the first a key player in the decriminalization. Drug usage as well as overdoses and HIV transmissions have gone down since 2001. The State of Oregon decriminalized all illicit drugs in 2006 and appears to have modeled their policy on the success of Portugal. In 2019 Illinois was the 11th state to legalize recreational marijuana. Whats obvious to me is that the federal government has no business prosecuting people for substances. By prohibition of Cannabis for example the government is essentially calling all

American's complete idiots. Inferring that no man or woman legally an adult can possibly use this substance safely without endangering others. This is obviously not the case. It should be up to the states. Amendment X of The Constitution states: "The powers not delegated to the United States by the Constitution, nor prohibited by it to the States, are reserved to the States respectively, or to the people.". Portugal has proven that criminalizing illicit drugs is a matter of opinion not necessity. I believe in the general rule of law that a mere opinion without necessity doesn't belong in law especially on a federal level. It discredits law entirely to have unjustified laws. "People have an absolute right to put whatever they want in their bodies because their bodies belong to them", Roger Ver CEO of Bitcoin.com.

I have always prided myself on not being dependent on anything. Not drugs legal or illicit. Not alcohol. I like to drink occasionally. Scientologist reject all drugs because they interfere with a persons capability to think rationally. They also think the pharmaceutical industry is a for-profit conspiracy. I believe in physical therapy and in avoiding surgery. I believe in health and strength. Once, I suspected a dentist of lying when he claimed I had several cavities. I then had consultations with two other dentists. All three dentists said completely different things. The last one said I was 100% good and didn't need to see a dentist for another year. If you can't see or feel a cavity it's probably not there. William Ecenbarger, a writer, reported he had seen fifty dentists across the U.S. in 2020 and said he received a different diagnosis from almost every dentist. A lot of the medical field is like this but not all. Psychiatry is a sham. Surgeons sell surgery and dentist sell crowns and fillings..

The Supreme Court of the United States ruled a federal tax payer has grounds to challenge government's unconstitutional misuse of those funds. "Appellant taxpayers allege that federal funds have been disbursed by appellee federal officials under the Elementary and Secondary Education Act of 1965 to finance instruction and the purchase of educational materials for use in religious and sectarian school, in violation of the Establishment and Free Exercise Clauses of the First Amendment. Appellants sought a declaration that the expenditures were not authorized by the Act or, in the alternative, that the Act is to that extent unconstitutional, and requested the convening of a three-judge court". That three-judge panel dismissed the complaint with one dissenting judge. Chief Justice Warren delivered the opinion of the Court. "The Complaint alleged that the seven appellants had as a common attribute that 'each pays income taxes of the United States,' and it is clear from the complaint that the appellants were resting their standing to maintain the action solely on their status as federal taxpayers... For reasons explained at length below, we hold that appellants do have standing as federal taxpayers to maintain this action, and the judgment below must be reversed", See Flast v. Cohen, 392 U.S. 83 (1968). Actors make great politicians. Jesse Venture was a pro wrestler who was elected governor of Minnesota in 1998. In 1991 he was elected as mayor of Brooklyn Park, Minnesota. Before his political career he dropped out of North Hennepin Community College. Arnold Alois Schwarzenegger was elected as a Republican governor of California in 2003 and reelected in 2007. He has a college degree in business administration and marketing. Ronald Reagan was president of the Screen Actors Guild before he was President of the United States. He had a college degree from Eureka college in Illinois. Ronald Reagan was one of our greatest Republican Presidents who was reelected and served two terms. If you're strapped for cash the courts will waive your fees. Federal filing fees are about $400. State Courts cost a bit less.

In a free America, there is infinite potential to be all you can be. The sky is the limit for every man. Laws are necessary in modern society because they protect the civilized from the animals. They give you freedom to pursue your ambitions at the speed you wish. This is a rational basis for the laws that regulate society. Men under corrupt government are essentially slaves. Subject to, or to the potential of living under the will of other men. Every Man is a man. Pursuing your life by the discretion of other men is an atrocious insult to your purpose on this earth. A true man an American Man has no one between him and the sky. It is necessary for us to create rules we can agree to live by and those who break these rules must pay a price.

Winston Johnson was awarded compensatory damages by a jury in the U.S. District Court for emotional pain and mental anguish after being unlawfully detained by Barnes & Noble Booksellers security personnel. "Johnson's lawsuit arose from an incident at a Barnes & Noble store while he was there to purchase a compact disk and a book. At trial, Johnson testified that after purchasing the compact disk, he asked a female clerk for assistance in locating the book. As the store clerk stooped down to retrieve a book from the bottom of the shelf, she, or her shirt, was touched by Johnson. Johnson claimed that he was merely trying to help the store clerk with her shirt, which she was trying to reach in order to tuck it in, while the store clerk maintained that Johnson inappropriately grabbed her buttocks. The store clerk left Johnson and reported to her supervisors that Johnson had touched her inappropriately. Although not having observed the incident, two store managers and a security guard approached Johnson, accused him of having touched the store employee inappropriately, which Johnson adamantly denied, and then escorted Johnson to an office where he was detained for one to two hours. During this detention, he was interrogated, photographed and subjected to racially discriminatory remarks. When the police arrived, they questioned Johnson about the incident, returned his ID and driver's license, which had been taken from him by the Barnes & Noble employees, and told him to leave the store. Johnson was not arrested... Johnson subsequently filed suit against Barnes & Noble, claiming false imprisonment. The jury returned a verdict, finding Barnes & Noble liable for falsely imprisoning Johnson and awarding Johnson $117,000 for about an hour of unlawful detainment. In a post-verdict motion for a new trial, Barnes & Noble argued that the jury was erroneously instructed and that the verdict was excessive. The district court upheld the jury's verdict and denied the motion for a new trial. Barnes & Noble now appeals". The arrest was illegal because Florida law requires that in order to make a citizen's arrest for a misdemeanor, a person must have committed an offense in the presence of the person making the arrest however, Johnson was detained by security who did not witness the alleged crime. The United States Court of appeals, Eleventh Circuit ruled the United States District Court "did not err in denying the requested instruction" and "Based on all the relevant factors, we find that the award of $117,000 in this case was within the range of permissible awards and we cannot say that the award is 'so inordinately large as obviously to exceed the maximum limit of a reasonable range within which the jury may properly operate.' Accordingly, the jury's verdict is AFFIRMED". See Johnson v. Barnes & Noble Booksellers Inc.,437 F.3d 1112 (11th Cir. 2006).

I have two ideas for TV shows. One, is about a Film Producer in Los Angeles. I would like to play the Film Producer. Think Californication or Entourage. The other, is an outdoor talk show which I will host. The guests can be primarily Celebrities, actors, pro athletes and politicians. We will do various outdoor activities like trap shooting, fishing, wake boarding, golf, Kite boarding and scuba diving. I had in my vehicle at the time of the accident all the equipment necessary to start Filming pilots for either of these shows. Much of the equipment was damaged. I would to start rebuilding the production set. I had at the time of unlawful arrest $7,000 of

Filming equipment in my vehicle. Some of which went missing like my external hard drive. I also have considered making a documentary about the case in Arizona similar to *The Murder of Lacey Peterson* (2017) with Nancy Grace and Larry King.

According to Professor Jordan Peterson the "Big Five" predictors of success after IQ are: Extroversion, emotional stability, agreeableness, conscientiousness and openness. I am an extrovert, I like to work with people. I am emotionally stable. I am agreeable. I am Conscientious. And I am an open person open to new ideas and to discussion. I agree that freedom of speech is under attack by the left who also hate the Bible because it condemns homosexuality. Emotions are the antonym of logic. One who seeks to discern logic from emotion undertakes an endless endeavor. I like to listen to Jordan Peterson as I like to listen to Candace Owens. I also usually agree with Ron Paul.

I'd like to see this book brings about new opportunities. I'd like to work anywhere in California or in Washington D.C.. I'd like to get invited to celebrity parties. I'd like to work with the Big Tech companies. I am interested in internships. I would like to intern with the Media, on TV productions, on major Hollywood productions and and with any big company doing marketing and sales. I have been applying for jobs as a Journalist with all the major News Networks. I'd like to intern with executives. I would like to intern as an Assistant Director or Production Assistant. I would like to intern at a Talent Agency or with a Production Company. I will intern at a Law Firm. I would like to intern with a Lobby group or on a Campaign. At the very least I will be able to write about it in the future or it will help me as an Actor. Please do send me offers and invitations I think I should be guaranteed a career in Entertainment and politics after writing this and speaking on TV for almost fifteen minutes like no man before me. I like to play the lead but enjoy cameos. I want to play CEOs, Politicians, Professors, Coaches, Doctors, Captains, Pilots, Professional Athletes, Military and more. I want to be in movies that tell a great story or send a message. I want to work with talented directors. I want a bigger Talent Agency. I want to make movies with Clint Eastwood and Quentin Tarantino. I studied Public Speaking in College I will Host The Emmys, The Grammies and The Oscars.

Civic Duties include respecting the rights of others and being mindful of government conduct. This Book is already longer than the Book that got Trump elected. I would like to release the book as soon as possible. It is a Civic Duty to support people's presumption of innocence and their right to release on reasonable bail. It's a "Civic Duty" to do a little research on law and politics and to vote for candidates who's policies aren't reckless. Arizona dismissed the charges because they ruled I was incompetent to stand trial. I Aced Abnormal Psychology in College. State level government employees of basic intelligence are preventing geniuses from asserting their constitutional rights and making a defense by alleging incompetence. This is Unacceptable. They can't call people crazy because they feel stupid. It was an astronomical assault on the Constitution and the security of the public in a national Media case. They essentially ruled that the Constitutional protections didn't apply to me. There is no exemption from the constitution, it applies equally to everyone. This was a violation of Equal Protections of Law explicit in the Fourteenth Amendment. According to memory and aptitude tests I'm more competent than most of the population so what does this mean for people of average intelligence? Does the government now think the majority of the population can be deprived of liberty or property their without due process of law? It's peoples Civic Duty to keep the government in check. It is a Civic Duty to condemn police assault. I've been to jail illegally twice. The Cover Photo was taken before I was ever in jail. My youthful acting career was stolen from me for doing nothing unjustified or illegal. I was in my prime and I could have had a career like Brad Pitt. I moved to Hollywood about the same age he did and I did as well if not better than he did in my first year. The media preclusion order was entirely unjustified and contrary to the founding principles of our country. It was unconstitutional. The U.S. Supreme Court has ruled the priority is the defendant's rights of due process and impartiality of the jury in cases with media coverage. The Supreme Court of the United States also ruled a media preclusion order was unconstitutional in a case where the defendant even requested it, See Nebraska Press Association v. Stuart, 427 US 539 (1976). It was a Civic Duty and a duty of the press and public to object to an illegal media preclusion order or other illegal government conduct. This case represents a tremendous injustice and a failure of the public's Civic Duties. It's also people's Civic Duty to make sure people are compensated if their Civil Rights have been violated. We must fix these problems we all face so we can get back to supreme exaltation.

We need Civilian oversight Committees for law enforcement. We need to review the convictions standards to prevent unjustified prosecutions. We need to end qualified immunity. We need to end judicial immunity. We need to prosecute law enforcement for excessive force and especially for use of unconstitutional deadly force. We need to enforce the law equally and indiscriminately. We need to enforce Supreme Court of the United States law with the Civil Rights Act. Don't have blind faith in big government. Value your rights. Defend Due Process of Law and Defend our right to privacy from government. Read Supreme Court Law. Read the Constitution. Defend the Constitution. Defend Liberty. Fulfill some Civic Duties. Enjoy your Pursuit of Happiness! You're invited to explore my website www.MitchTaebel.com! Please share this Book!

Made in the USA
Columbia, SC
22 October 2021

47638725R00102